CAREERS IN FILM AND TELEVISION

So You Want to Work in Work in Set Design, Costuming, or Make-Up?

Torene Svitil and Amy Dunkleberger

E **Enslow Publishers, Inc.**
40 Industrial Road
Box 398
Berkeley Heights, NJ 07922
USA

http://www.enslow.com

Library of Congress Cataloging-in-Publication Data

Svitil, Torene.
    So you want to work in set design, costuming, or make-up? / Torene Svitil and Amy
    Dunkleberger.
        p. cm. — (Careers in film and television)
    Summary: "Details how to become a set designer, costume designer, or make-up artist for film
    and television"—Provided by publisher.
    Includes bibliographical references and index.
    ISBN-13: 978-0-7660-2740-4
    ISBN-10: 0-7660-2740-6
    1. Motion pictures—Setting and scenery—Vocational guidance—Juvenile literature.
    2. Costume—Vocational guidance—Juvenile literature. 3. Film makeup—Vocational
    guidance—Juvenile literature. I. Dunkleberger, Amy. II. Title.
    PN1995.9.S4S85 2008
    791.4302023—dc22

                                    2007022364

Printed in the United States of America

10 9 8 7 6 5 4 3 2 1

To Our Readers:
We have done our best to make sure all Internet addresses in this book were active and appropriate
when we went to press. However, the author and the publisher have no control over and assume no
liability for the material available on those Internet sites or on other Web sites they may link to.
Any comments or suggestions can be sent by e-mail to comments@enslow.com or to the
address on the back cover.

Illustration Credits: All images courtesy of the Everett Collection, Inc.

Cover Illustration: Shutterstock.

CONTENTS

INTRODUCTION

The focus of this book is art direction, one of the major elements of filmmaking. Headed by production designers and complemented by costume designers and make-up and hair artists, the art direction team is a diverse but vital component of movie-making. They provide the visual backdrop over which an entire film story plays. Through art direction, filmmakers can quickly tell the audience the who, what, where, and when of storytelling—and sometimes even the how.

PRODUCTION DESIGN— FROM STAGE TO SCREEN

William Cameron Menzies, who created the epic Technicolor look of *Gone With the Wind* (1939), is considered the father of modern production design. The first art director to receive an Academy Award, Menzies' ideas went beyond set building and decorating into the realm of costume design and special effects. His extraordinary cinematic vision and unique personal style on such films as *The Dove* (1928) and Alfred Hitchcock's *Foreign Correspondent* (1940) helped give the art director's position prestige in Hollywood.

Today, production designers oversee large crews and big budgets. Some production designers do all or most of their work off-set, preferring to concentrate on

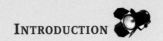

the conceptual end of art direction, while assigning the day-to-day tasks to their crew.

COSTUMES AND MAKE-UP

In 1914, Max Factor created the first make-up for movies. Factor's design compensated for the fact that high contrast black-and-white film stock made natural skin tones appear darker than normal, and reds, oranges, and browns look black, while blues, pinks, and yellows appear white. As film stock Improved and acting become more natural, make-up became lighter and longer-lasting.

In the 1930s and 1940s, film studios maintained huge costume departments and a large costume stock. By the 1960s, only a few studios still maintained costume departments. Despite the disbandment of costume departments and the trend for using ready-made garments, costume designers draw a distinction between fashion and costumes. As costume designer Sandy Powell states: "The most important thing about costume design, and the most exciting part, is helping create a character and contribute to a story. It's not about how glamorous, or sexy, or wonderful somebody looks. It's about making the character."[1]

1

PRODUCTION DESIGN

Movies and television are visual media. From the first pages of the screenplay to the final cut of the print, the objective of filmmaking is to tell stories through moving pictures. Screenwriters begin the process of visual imagining through their choice of time and place, and the specific way they move their characters within a physical world. Directors then make the writer's vision their own, overseeing the realization of that physical world in specific cinematic terms.

During production, directors have two all-important collaborators—the production designer and the cinematographer. The cinematographer devises the photographic look of a movie and films the story's action. The production designer, sometimes called the art director, creates the physical world behind the action, as interpreted by the director.

Designer Lawrence G. Paull (*Blade Runner*, *Back to the Future*) describes movie design simply as "an arena in which the actors and the director interact and play a scene out."[1] Stuart Wurtzel (*Hannah and Her Sisters*; *Charlotte's Web*) adds that the role of the film designer is to devise "a visual and emotional world for the story to unfold."[2]

STEP ONE: THE SCREENPLAY

Like all film collaborators, production designers begin their job by reading the screenplay thoughtfully, taking notes and discussing the story's premise with the director. A good designer always puts the needs of the story and the director's vision first. As Oscar-winning designer Paul Sylbert (*Heaven Can Wait; Conspiracy Theory*) notes, "Design is not self-expression. It is an expressive use of object, forms, and colors in the service of the script."[3]

Generally speaking, the script will mention only those physical details that are especially relevant to the scene. For example, a script might indicate that a scene set in a college dorm room contains a bust of Edgar Allan Poe, if the student's love of Poe is a significant character or plot point. The script is less likely to describe how big the room is, whether it has curtains or rugs, or if there are numerous coffee stains on the desk. Those details are the responsibility of the production designer.

In all likelihood, the production designer in the above example will include the Poe bust in his or her design, then add all the other details, selecting them based on the dramatic needs of the scene. The designer might decide, for instance, that the walls should be painted black to emphasize the student's obsession with death, or that the room should be cramped and tomb-like.

The first and most important question for the production designer is: How can I use my skills and artistry to best serve the script? In his book, *What an Art Director Does*, designer Ward Preston notes, "Just as a composer can use tempo to induce tension or a minor key to convey sadness, the designer has in his vocabulary the visual tools to induce emotions. It is the designer's ability to manipulate visual associations that sets the style of a well-designed film."[4]

ESTABLISHING A STYLE

Before production designers draw their first serious sketch, they will determine with the director an overall design style for a movie. Will the look be warm and realistic, or dark and surreal? Monotone or multi-colored? An urban murder mystery, for example, might call for down-and-dirty monotone realism, while a romance might demand a warmer, softer approach.

Comedies sometimes feature exaggerated styles, as do science fiction and fantasy movies. For example, the design style of the *Pirates of the Caribbean* trilogy mixes a straight historical look with exaggerated fantasy elements. The late seventeenth, early eighteenth century period is established with recogniz-able accuracy, but many of the settings—the haunted ships in particular—have bizarre, exaggerated touches.

Working directly under the production designer to make the chosen style a reality are the costume and make-up designers. Although costume and make-up people have their own crews, their creative decision-making must mesh with the director and production designer's scheme for a film. Some of these decisions are subtle and may go unnoticed by the casual viewer. The filmmakers know, however, that every detail within a setting has the potential to influence the audience's perception of the story.

The tattered black sails emphasize the supernatural elements of the ship in Pirates of the Caribbean: The Curse of the Black Pearl *(2003).*

ARCHITECTURE

Good art direction, like good architecture, requires a solid knowledge of building fundamentals. Discussing the architectural nature of his work, television production designer John Iacovelli (*The Old Settler*) says, "What we use as designers is a series of tools. It's like a language. We start with thumbnail sketches, asking 'How big could this set be?' . . . That's when I kind of become an architect for a few days. I'll sit down with

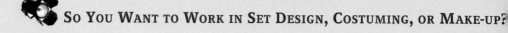

the amount of room that we have onstage, move things, and create the ideal ground plan."[5]

VOLUME AND SCALE

Included in the "language" of architectural design are the volume, shape, scale, and depth of a proposed space. Volume, the total size of a space, is probably the most basic and obvious architectural feature of production design. Sometimes the size of a space is dictated by the setting itself. In many other instances, however, the production designer chooses size based

John Cusack and Mary Kay Price in the 1999 film Being John Malkovich.

on the specific emotional or thematic needs of a scene.

An extreme example of size manipulation occurs in *Being John Malkovich* (1999). For scenes set in the film's mysterious "seven-and-a-half floor," designer K. K. Barrett created office rooms with very low ceilings that forced the actors to bend over while walking. The literal squashing of the characters echoed the emotional pressure the main character was feeling at that point in the story.

Related to size is scale, or the relative size of objects within a setting. Scale can also be manipulated for dramatic effect. Characters who are overwhelmed or fearful, for instance, might be placed in an oversized room that underscores their insecurity. When terrified Dorothy goes to see the wizard for the first time in *The Wizard of Oz* (1939), she appears dwarfed by the huge palace hall she must cross to reach him.

SHAPE AND DEPTH

Like volume, the shape of a setting can hint at emotional states. Entrapment might be suggested by a box-like set, similar to a prison cell. Conversely, a rounded or curved space appears softer and more inviting than a square or rectangular space.

Depth in a set refers to how far back into a setting the viewer can potentially see and, as with other architectural elements, can be employed for dramatic effect. Like a painting, a set's depth can be enhanced through perspective. Perspective is the illusion of depth, as rendered on a two-dimensional surface, such as a movie screen. For budgetary and even artistic reasons, designers sometimes must find creative ways to produce a very large, deep space out of a small area. Collaborating with Alfred Hitchcock, Robert Boyle became proficient at "cheating" shots through design: "You're achieving a large space in a limited space. You bring background up, and you force everything smaller."[6]

Windows and doors increase the appearance of depth on a set and are a favorite designer tool. Many television shows, particularly ones like *The Office* and *Without a Trace*, which revolve around a work place, feature glass partitions in their design scheme. Glass partitions separate characters realistically—the boss's office is distinct from the underlings'—while at the same time allowing the audience to connect the characters visually from scene to scene.

COLOR AND TEXTURE

Along with architectural elements, production designers rely on color and texture to make their vision come alive. During pre-production, designers will devise color and fabric palettes for the main characters in a script. Palettes include fabric swatches and color chips—similar to color strips found in any paint store. The various colors and materials are then posted on a board for use by various members of the art department.

Color in production design serves many purposes. Because everyone learns about and uses color from an early age, it is perhaps the designer's most obvious and accessible tool. Color helps distinguish characters, and it can convey a sense of time and place. As with architectural elements of design, color is used to suggest emotional states, and it can help create mood and atmosphere.

Sometimes designers will assign a particular color to a character. In the *Legally Blonde* movies, for example, pink is Elle Woods' (Reese Witherspoon's) signature color. Character color can be echoed throughout a movie's design. A character who always

Reese Witherspoon as the pink-loving Elle Woods from 2001's Legally Blonde.

How Colors Work

Since colors are a significant element in all aspects of art direction, understanding their nature and how they work together is key for design success.

Red, orange, yellow, green, blue, and violet comprise the basic colors of the spectrum. Hues are combinations of the basic colors: red-orange, yellow-orange, yellow-green, blue-green, blue-violet, and red-violet. Although two colors are present in a hue, one color dominates to a lesser or greater degree. Orange, yellow, and red are considered warm hues. Blue, green, and violet are cool hues.

Value refers to how light or dark a hue appears when compared to neighboring hues on the spectrum. Adding white to a hue lightens its value, while adding black darkens it. A tint is a hue to which white has been added. By contrast, saturated colors are pure, with no white added. In black-and-white films, value becomes especially important, as production designers must translate colors into values between black and white, called the gray scale. The brightness of a color depends on its luminance, or how much light is reflected off of it.

When thinking about color choice, production designers must keep in mind how colors appear on film (as opposed to the naked eye). For example, a designer will know that any color will appear lighter when filmed against a black background, and vice-versa. Warm hues will appear closer to the camera than cool colors. Colors appear more saturated on smooth surfaces than on rough surfaces.

wears bright, outrageous colors will likely have brightly colored furniture and walls as well.

Color can also be used to underline contrast within a character's world. In *Nacho Libre* (2006), production designer Gideon Ponte made a sharp color contrast between Nacho's dull world at the orphanage, which was dominated by browns and other earth tones, and the bright colors of the neighboring town and the even brighter colors of the wrestling arenas he frequents.

TEXTURE AND MATERIALS

Textures display themselves in materials such as fabrics—curtains, rugs, and costumes—but also in walls, floors, and any other type of surface. Designers will pick texture and materials, along with colors, to bring out character personality traits, dramatic themes, atmosphere, and so on.

A room filled with smooth, shiny objects, like mirrors and stainless steel appliances, might suggest a bright, reflective personality. Or taken with other design elements, it might hint at a cold, unfeeling world. Walls boasting peeling paint and cracks immediately convey the feeling of neglect and possibly poverty.

Textures are often used to suggest age and wear-and-tear. In *Pirates of the Caribbean: Dead Man's Chest*, production designer Rick Heinricks and his crew made sure to "weather," or age, the bars in the island prison cells. Instead of smooth iron, the bars appear rough and rusted—aged.

SET DECORATION

The décor of a room is its overall style and is suggested primarily by the furniture. Common décors include modern, traditional, rustic, and European, but the décor of a specific set may be more haphazard or mixed. Although production designers oversee the decorating of a set, set decorators make the initial decisions regarding décor and furnishings.

Décor can be extremely effective at suggesting character, theme, and atmosphere. As Ward Preston observes, "A successfully dressed set or location should become as much a part of the actor's persona as the clothes on his back."[7]

CAMERA ANGLE AND MOVEMENT

When designing for the typical stage production, theater designers imagine the audience seeing their creation from fixed points in the auditorium. Set pieces may move around the stage, but the audience's perspective of them remains the same. With films, the viewer's perspective is ever changing. Shifting camera angles and movement make for a dynamic perspective.

Although the cinematographer is responsible for executing camera movements during a scene, the production designer always keeps camera placement and movement in mind while creating sets. Set design should not only accommodate angles and moving cameras—making sure furniture, walls, and doorways do not get in the way of the cameraman—but enhance it as well.

For instance, columns or other vertical pieces placed in the foreground will make a moving shot more visually dynamic. Similarly, strategic placement by the set decorator can draw the eye toward a particular object as the camera moves through a shot. To accentuate a high-angle shot—one looking down on a person or object—for example, special attention might be paid to a set's flooring or carpeting.

Sometimes the sets themselves can affect angle and be used for dramatic impact. Sections of sets can be artificially raised or lowered, or skewed at extreme angles. Ward Preston notes, "Elevation connotes superiority, holiness, isolation, chilliness, and vulnerability while depression [slope or dip] implies security, warmth, inferiority, and evil. The desk of a cunning executive might well be placed on a slightly raised platform, immediately putting his visitors at a disadvantage. Or, to give added intimacy to that recessed hearth-side inglenook, it can be placed a few steps below the level of the rest of the room."[8]

In addition to the moving camera, the decoration itself can move. Waving flags, fluttering curtains, falling leaves—all of these can add interest to a shot.

PRODUCTION DESIGN AND THE SMALL SCREEN

Designing for television involves many of the same aesthetic techniques used in features. In addition to time and budget constraints, however, television design has to take into consideration the size of the average viewing screen. According to Herman

The Design Department

Helping the production designer to create the physical world of the film is a large crew of artisans and technicians. Below are some of the key members of a typical art department team.

Art Director: The art director is the production designer's second-in-command, coordinating the day-to-day operations of the art department. Art directors often supervise activities on the set during filming, while the production designer remains off-set, designing and consulting with the director and cinematographer.

Set Designer: Based on the production designer's vision, the set designer plans and creates drawings used to construct specific sets, drafts blueprints, and oversees construction of the sets. The set designer reports to the art director.

Set Decorator: The set decorator is responsible for the décor of a set or location.

Leadman: Also known as the assistant set decorator, the leadman tracks down props, furniture, and other decorations used to dress a set.

Set Dresser: The set dresser works with the set decorator and oversees placing, or dressing, the décor on a set.

Swing Gang: Also known as the set dressing crew, the swing gang is in charge of the physical dressing of a set. Among the many items the swing gang might provide for a given set are light fixtures and electrical outlets, posters, bathroom accessories, rugs, and potted plants.

Property Master: The property master is responsible for acquiring any prop or object handled by the actors during the action of a scene.

Greensman: The greensman oversees the care, maintenance, and style of any greenery on a set or location—grass, shrubbery, flowers, trees, houseplants, and so on.

Construction Coordinator: The construction coordinator is directed artistically by the production designer and works with the set designer in executing drawings and blueprints. Movie construction coordinators are expert at building temporary edifices using inexpensive or imitation materials.

Construction Crew: The construction crew consists of many painters and carpenters. Like their coordinator, movie construction crew members are skilled at building and painting sets so they appear on film in a specific way.

Scenic Artist: The scenic artist creates painted backgrounds, signage, magazine or book covers, prop paintings, and any illustrative material required on a set.

Location Scout: In collaboration with the director and production designer, the location scout searches for places indicated in the script that will not be created on a soundstage.

Zimmerman, designer on many of the *Star Trek* television series, "The television format is smaller because the screen is smaller. The resolution is lower than film . . . and you can get away with less attention to detail. Conversely, instead of a 19" diagonal or even a 35" screen, the cinemascope screen can be 30' tall and 70' wide. And the images on it magnified hundreds of times more than the images on your television screen."[9]

Production designers are also aware that in television, where much of the story is told through dialogue, the camera tends to focus on the actors more than on the surrounding environment. Shots are composed to give the viewer as much visual information in as short a time as possible.

COSTUME AND MAKE-UP DESIGN

"**D**esigning really starts first with the script," states costume designer Deena Appel (*The Lake House*; the *Austin Powers* movies).[1] The script provides key information that affects designs and budgets, such as the number of actors, the location and time period of the film, and the action in each scene.

On a practical level, the script helps costume designers determine how many different costumes will be needed for each character and whether duplicate costumes will be required for stunts or other purposes.

Make-up artists and hairstylists note when the script calls for special make-up, including scenes where actors need to be older or younger than they are, action scenes with injuries or bullet wounds, and the presence of fantasy creatures such as werewolves or aliens from outer space.

COSTUME DESIGNERS

When costume designers analyze a script, they ask a series of questions: Who is in the scene? What happens in each scene? Where and under what conditions does each scene take place? When does the scene take place? What purpose does the scene serve in the film? How will the scene be shot?[2] The answers help them determine what the costumes should look like, whether they will be constructed or "built" by the costume crew or purchased in stores, how many costumes will be needed, and how their designs will fit into the film's budget.

The size of the crew is determined by the number and complexity of the costumes and the film's budget. A crew generally includes a costume supervisor, who manages and supervises the costume department's day-to-day operations; costumers, who dress the actors and maintain the costumes; and pattern-makers, seamstresses, and tailors, who build or alter the costumes. Sometimes a costume illustrator will come on board to draw the designs for presentation to the producer and director. Large productions might require knitters, shoe makers, jewelry makers, furriers, armorers, or other specialized craftspeople.

Who Is in the Scene?

A character's social status, age, nationality, profession, sexuality, religion, health, politics, education, and eccentricities influence the clothes he or she wears. As costume designer Sophie de Rakoff (*In Her Shoes*, *Legally Blonde*) puts it:

You have to understand who the characters are immediately, because until you understand who they are, you don't understand what they look like and how they dress and why they dress a certain way. . . . You have to understand what's going on inside of the script and the aim of the movie— what the tone is and what the theme is and what it's meant to be when it's finished.[3]

In *Legally Blonde 2: Red, White & Blonde*, Elle, an animal rights activist, wears animal-free clothing. For unemployed, nomadic party girl Maggie, Cameron Diaz's character in *In Her Shoes*, de Rakoff designed a body-revealing, stylish but inexpensive wardrobe that fits in the large garbage bag Maggie carries as an improvised suitcase.

What Happens in the Scene?

A scene at a prom requires different costumes than a scene that takes place during a bank robbery. Action scenes demand durable clothing and duplicate costumes for the stunt doubles. Clothing for a hunting party will have a different palette than that worn by people at a board meeting.

Where and When Does Each Scene Take Place?

Rural, urban, foreign, or local settings suggest different kinds of costumes. Costumes vary depending on whether the scene happens indoors or outdoors, if it is winter or summer, raining or snowing. If the scene calls for rain, multiple copies of the costumes are provided so that dry clothes will be available for re-takes. If a scene occurs in the snow, costume designers supply warm underwear and heavy socks to keep the actors comfortable during filming.

The film's historical setting, the season of the year, and the time of day, as well as the passage of time within the film must be considered. For films that cover several years, such as *When Harry Met Sally*, costumes help anchor each scene in the correct time period.

What Purpose Does the Scene Serve in the Film?

When a character goes through an emotional change, costumes can subtly cue the audience. A shirt that becomes slightly less buttoned up as the film progresses may indicate a softening of the character's temperament, for instance. A closer relationship between two characters may be signaled by putting them in clothes with a similar palette.

How Will the Scene Be Shot?

Designers also take into account the camera angles suggested in the script. A close-up shot calls for a costume that focuses attention on the actor's face. Special effects scenes are shot against a blue or green screen, an optical process that allows different elements to be combined in the computer. Because all blues or greens are removed from effects shots in post-production, designers avoid using those colors in special effects scenes.

New digital processes affect the way colors look in the finished film. A deep burgundy in real life may look as red as a tomato on screen. Designers working with new technologies depend on the cinematographer and special effects artists to help them choose the right colors.

Colors look different under indoor lighting than they do in natural outdoor light. White, for example, needs to be yellower when the scene takes place outdoors because sunlight has a brightening effect.

Color, Line, Shape, and Texture

Working within the palette chosen by the production designer and director, costume designers use color to express characters' emotions and create moods. In *In Her Shoes,* de Rakoff reflects the characters' unhappy lives in New York by dressing them in muted shades. By contrast, in sunny Florida, the clear blues, corals, and yellows they wear symbolize their increasing self-confidence.

Line, whether vertical, horizontal, diagonal, curved, or straight, is found in fabric patterns, seams, and other design elements and in the garment's fit. Designers use line to focus attention, to make actors look taller or slimmer, and to express emotion. For example, broken lines suggest conflict or activity. Long vertical lines, on the other hand, indicate elegance or power.

Together with line and color, the shape of a costume can disguise or enhance an actor's body or reveal aspects of character. In their book *Costuming for Film: The Art and the Craft*, Kristin Burke and Holly Cole

In the 2005 movie, In Her Shoes, *Toni Collette plays an attorney whose change in wardrobe mirrors the character's transformation.*

explain, "Tailored shapes . . . evoke a feeling of power and authority. Shapes that hug and reveal the body can be sexy. Garments that expose the neck and shoulders can create a feeling of vulnerability. . . . Shapes that create an odd silhouette . . . can seem funny."[4] Shapes change depending on the movie's time period—from the soft drapery of the Roman era, to the body-concealing garments of the Victorians, to the miniskirts and geometric silhouettes of the 1960s.

Texture is the way fabric feels to the touch and looks to the eye. It ranges from rough wools to translucent, smooth silks. "Pointy collars, crisp clothes, and suits read as armor. Stretchy, knit clothes read as more vulnerable," says costume designer Jane Ruhm (*Tracey Takes On*; *Matilda*).[5]

Creating Character With Costume

The right costumes help actors create their characters. For *The Addams Family*, designer Ruth Meyers put actress Anjelica Huston into a corset and a skin-tight black dress. The costume forced Huston to walk in a controlled but sexy manner that perfectly suited eccentric Morticia Addams.

Once the actors have been cast, the designer must also consider their body shapes and how to play down their flaws and play up their best features.

Aging, Distressing, Duplicate Costumes

In real life, clothes do not look as if they came straight from the department store, so before they appear on screen, costumes might be dyed slightly or airbrushed to make them seem lived in.

Garments that are supposed to be old, such as those that have belonged to a character for years, are subjected to a more rigorous aging process, known as distressing.

> **DISTRESSING—**
> Dyeing, sanding, airbrushing, and otherwise treating costumes so that they look old.

Dyeing is the first step in distressing a costume. Seams, pockets, cuffs, and colors are shaded to show wear, and natural creases are deepened. Garments may be washed and sanded multiple times, or they may be torn or ripped. "Schmutz" sticks (pigmented earth with a wax binder,) may be used to make clothes look muddy or dirty. Mineral oil and glycerin can be rubbed in to make sweat stains.

Time passage is shown by progressively aging duplicate costumes. In *Gone with the Wind*, actress Vivien Leigh wore many versions of the same dress. During scenes depicting the burning of Atlanta, she changed her dress multiple times, starting with a dress in perfect condition and ending with one that was filthy and ripped.

Identical duplicate costumes are kept on hand if the film calls for action that might damage costumes, or for rain, snow, or other severe weather. Duplicate costumes are prepared for stunt doubles, actors who perform hazardous actions in place of the film's stars.

MAKE-UP

Every character in a movie wears make-up, whether the movie is set in the present day with regular people (straight and beauty make-up), in the Middle Ages (period make-up), or on a planet far, far away (fantasy and special effects make-up). If the script calls for actors to age over the course of a movie or to play someone older or younger than they actually are, it requires age make-up.

Make-up artists construct false noses or other features, called prosthetics or appliances, to make actors look like a well-known person or an imaginary creature. They are responsible for attaching scars and bullet wounds and placing blood.

According to make-up artist Greg Nicotero, the best make-up is one that the viewer does not notice: "People don't go, 'Wait a minute. Mickey Rourke's in a make-up. Bruce Willis is in a make-up. Nick Stahl's in a make-up.' You don't think about it because you're so busy watching the film. To me, that's a compliment because I don't want people pulled out of the film. I want them to be absorbed into it.[6]

Make-up is affected by the lighting in each scene and the format, whether color, black and white, or digital. Intense lighting on a television or movie set washes out color, so to compensate, make-up artists work with warmer shades.

Television
Make-up for television programs can reflect current fashions more than make-up for a film, which might not be released until after styles have changed. Hairstyles on television programs tend to be larger and more

exaggerated than those in films, because it is harder to see detail on the smaller screen.

Television shows do not have the luxury of long shooting schedules, so television make-up has to be completed quickly. "If anyone's in the chair more than forty-five minutes, it's almost too long," says Steve LaPorte, make-up artist on *Lost*.[7]

High definition (HD) digital video, which is very revealing, requires special attention. Even the lightest traditional make-up can look too heavy. Make-up for HD works best when it is translucent and slightly reflective. Hairstylists strive for natural looks because hairstyles that are too stiff or shiny look fake when shot with HD video.

> ## PROSTHETICS—
> Materials, including foam, latex, rubber, plastic, and gelatin, that are molded and applied to the face or body to change their shape or appearance. They can be as small as a nosepiece or as large as entire suits.

Creating Character With Make-up and Hair Design

Although make-up designers may have a clear concept for a character, the director, production designer, costume designer, cinematographer, and the actor will all have their own ideas of what each character should look like. As make-up artist Kevin Haney points out:

> A director can use artistic, creative choice to make a woman in a period picture look prettier by using a more modern approach. For example,

Faye Dunaway in *Bonnie and Clyde* (1967) or Madonna in *Dick Tracy* (1990). Directors Arthur Penn, and Warren Beatty didn't want them to have a period look, they just wanted them to look good.[8]

An actor's facial structure, features, skin tones, and hair color determine what and how make-up is applied. Dark clothing makes make-up look lighter and the opposite is also true. Make-up artists also consider how a face looks against the film's sets and background.

Straight Make-up

Also known as "street" make-up, straight make-up must look natural in sunlight or artificial light, from close up and from a distance. It must suit the character as well as flatter the actor. Whether an actor is playing an ordinary woman or a gang member, the make-up should be appropriate to the character.

Foundation, the first layer of make-up, evens out facial coloring and covers blemishes and beard stubble. The best foundation has a natural tone that will complement the actor's complexion and also photograph well.

Contouring can diminish a large chin or create the flattering illusion of cheekbones. Shading is used to

> **FOUNDATION—**
> A skin-colored, light-reflecting make-up that provides a base for color and contouring.

> **CONTOURING—**
> The application of shades and colors to the face or body to define or subtly change shapes.

33

contour the face in a black-and-white film. But because shading makes the actor look dirty when photographed with color film, layers of color are used instead. Reflective make-up helps diminish shadows, such as those often found under eyes. Pale lashes and brows may be colored or hairpieces used to fill out thinning hair.

Beauty Make-up

Simply put, beauty make-up, a type of straight make-up, makes stars look gorgeous. It is designed to highlight the actresses' best and most important features while downplaying their less attractive traits. Because eyes are the most communicative features, most beauty make-up emphasizes them.

Character Make-up

Character make-up is "the application of make-up to change the appearance of a person as to age, race, characteristics, or facial and/or body form."[9] Character make-up becomes more complex when the actor portrays an actual person, or when the same actor plays multiple characters in one film. Complex make-up takes longer to prepare, including time for research, testing, and sometimes manufacturing make-up or appliances.

Age Make-up

As people age, skin changes color, loses elasticity, and sags into bags, jowls, and pouches. Natural expression lines deepen. Skull bones become thinner. Faces either lose volume, making the ears appear larger, or they acquire extra fat deposits.

Aging a younger actor can be as simple as thinning and graying the hair and applying an old-age stipple, or as complex as adding prosthetics, appliances, contact lenses, wigs, hairpieces, and false teeth.

Old-age stipple, developed by George Bau during the 1950s, is a mixture of gum latex, powder, gelatin, and ground-up pancake make-up. When applied to skin with a coarse sponge and dried, it can be stretched to produce realistic wrinkles and rough skin textures.

Beards and other facial hair can disguise a youthfully firm chin area, and old-fashioned glasses serve the dual purpose of hiding the eye area and creating an impression of weakened eyesight. Age spots and veins may be painted in at the end.

> **OLD−AGE STIPPLE—**
> A mixture of gum latex, powder, gelatin, and ground-up pancake make-up. It can be dried and stretched to produce realistic wrinkles and rough skin textures to make actors appear older than they are.

Several different techniques can simulate baldness. A thin, plastic appliance called a bald cap, either alone or covered with a partial hairpiece, is one common method. Shaving the actor's head, if he is willing, saves time in the make-up chair. Lightening the edge of the hairline gives an impression of a receding hairline.

Age make-up techniques are also used to make actors look younger in flashbacks, as Russell Crowe does in *A Beautiful Mind*, or when a film covers a wide

Lon Chaney, the Man of a Thousand Faces

The actor Lon Chaney (1883–1930) was known as "the man of a thousand faces" for his skill in creating different characters through make-up. In the early days of filmmaking, he adapted theatrical make-up techniques and materials to make them more effective

Lon Chaney as Quasimodo in 1923's **The Hunchback of Notre Dame.**

onscreen. Chaney's make-ups remain powerful despite being created with relatively unsophisticated products.

Chaney often played two different characters in the same film, using make-up to distinguish between them. In the 1921 film *Outside the Law*, for example, he played both the criminal, Black Mike Silva, and Ah Wing, a Chinese man. At the end of the film Chaney, as Ah Wing, murders Chaney, as Black Mike.

To create his Chinese make-up, Chaney used materials such as fish skin, a thin, transparent skin intended for medical purposes, adhesive, and a black wig.

In the 1926 film *The Road to Mandalay*, he wore a glass eyepiece similar to a modern contact lens to create the appearance of a blind eye.

One of Chaney's most famous creations was Quasimodo, *The Hunchback of Notre Dame*. He devised a twenty-pound plaster hump held on by a leather harness that also prevented him from standing up straight. He built up his cheeks with layers of cotton and flexible collodian, a liquid plastic protective coating. He then covered everything with greasepaint. For a scene where Quasimodo is whipped on his bare back, he wore a flesh-like rubber shirt covered with crepe-wool hair.

Chaney specialized in people with monstrous faces, but he always emphasized each character's human qualities. "A man's face reveals much that is in his mind and heart. I attempt to show this by the make-up I use, and the make-up is merely the prologue."[10]

time span, like *Seabiscuit.* Lifts hidden in the actor's hair may be used for a temporary face lift, or appliances added to recreate a youthfully rounded profile.

In the 2006 movie *Click*, the characters age from eighteen to eighty. Special effects make-up artist Rick Baker used gelatin, silicone appliances, and old-age stipple on different actors.[11]

Both Julie Kavner and Henry Winkler, who play the parents of Adam Sandler's character, were also made up to look younger than their real ages with lifts and wigs. Baker experimented with silicone appliances for their youth make-up, but "when we did the make-ups, they just looked like ventriloquist dummies or something," Baker says.[12]

For the many flashbacks on the television program *Lost*, make-up artist Steve LaPorte uses different wigs and other appliances. "I had to shave [one actor] completely down for flashbacks, then hand lay his beard and mustache back on and then as it slowly grew out, start adding to it to keep it full," he recalled in an interview.[13]

Blood, Wounds, Scars, Gunshots

The corpses seen on television crime shows such as the *CSI* series or *Crossing Jordan* are created by special effects make-up artists. For an exotic dancer burned by a 1,000 degree sunlamp, *CSI* effects make-up artist John Goodwin created a six-piece overlapping gelatin make-up.

Because *Lost*'s storyline continues over many episodes, Steve LaPorte makes sure that wounds and scratches seen in one episode appear to heal gradually over several weeks.

Digital Enhancement

Many flaws that are normally covered with make-up can now be digitally removed in post-production. Wrinkles, tattoos, bad complexions, and even body contours can be corrected with computer software, and unflattering colors can be altered.

Computer graphics (CG) increasingly supplement traditional make-up. In *Harry Potter and the Goblet of Fire*, for instance, special make-up designer Nick Dudman determined that make-up and appliances alone could not create the look he wanted for Ralph Fiennes' villainous character Voldemort. Instead, he used CG to digitally reshape Fiennes' nose, flattening it and adding snake-like slits.

3

PUTTING IT ALL TOGETHER

PERIOD FILM:

Many production, costume, and make-up designers will say that creating the look of a period film is their favorite assignment. Certainly production and costume designers receive the greatest notice for their work on historical pictures. In just the last twenty years or so, all but a few Art Direction and Costume Design Academy Awards have gone to designers of period films.

During the silent period, historical films were all but synonymous with lavish art direction. Called "spectacles," these period films wowed audiences with the size and scope of their sets and costumes. Examples of early spectacles include the 1913 Italian films *Les Miserables* and *Quo Vadis* and D. W. Griffith's *Intolerance* (1916). The sets for *Intolerance*, built by carpenter Frank "Huck" Wortman and his crew, included full-scale recreations of ancient Babylon and sixteenth-century France. The Babylon feast scene sets remain some of the largest and most expensive in movie-making history.

Technicolor period epics like *Gone With the Wind* (1939) and *Ben-Hur* (1959) and more recent releases like *Braveheart* (1995) and *Gladiator* (2000) continued the "spectacle" movie tradition. Vital to these films' effectiveness is their lavish, detailed art direction. Even smaller period films like *Shakespeare in Love* (1998), *A Beautiful Mind* (2001), and *Seabiscuit* (2003), however, need razor-sharp art direction to bring their time and place to believable life.

SHAKESPEARE IN LOVE

The 1998 period comedy *Shakespeare in Love* was a surprise big-winner at the 71st Academy Awards, reeling in seven Oscars, including Best Picture and Best Original Screenplay. For their work on the film, production designer Martin Childs and set decorator Jill Quertier won the Best Art Direction prize, and Sandy Powell won for Best Costumes. Make-up and hair designers Veronica Brebner and Lisa Westcott earned an Oscar nomination.

Set in 1593, *Shakespeare in Love* is a fanciful look at the early career of the revered English playwright. Little is known about Shakespeare's life (even his actual identity is disputed by some historians), so screenwriters Marc Normand and Tom Stoppard felt free to invent and embellish. Their screen story mimics the structure of many of Shakespeare's comedies, containing disguises, mistaken identities, and gender switching.

The Story

At the start of their story Shakespeare (Joseph Fiennes) is nearly broke and suffering from severe writer's block, unable to begin his next play. At the same time, Viola De Lessep (Gwyneth Paltrow), a wealthy lord's daughter, yearns to be an actress, despite laws that forbid women from appearing on stage. Viola especially admires the work of Shakespeare and disguises herself as a man in order to audition for his proposed comedy, *Romeo and Ethel, the Pirate's Daughter.*

Unaware that talented would-be actor "Thomas Kent" is Viola in disguise, Shakespeare casts her as Romeo. When Shakespeare later meets Viola undisguised, he falls for her beauty and intelligence. He soon discovers her secret identity, and the two begin a clandestine affair. While Viola continues to rehearse as Romeo, Shakespeare completes his play, scene by scene.

Their love, doomed because Shakespeare is already married and Viola has been forcefully engaged to the brutish Lord Wessex (Colin Firth), inspires Shakespeare to write the tragic but stunning *Romeo and Juliet.*

Production Design

For English production designer Martin Childs, *Shakespeare in Love* proved both an extreme challenge and a wonderful artistic opportunity. The challenge came in recreating a specific four-hundred-year-old world familiar to many viewers—Elizabethan London and its theaters.

Childs took the same approach to the material, as did the screenwriters. While historical accuracy was important, imagination and playfulness ruled the day. "I had this mantra going in my head all the time," Childs recalled, "that this is not a documentary, we are allowed to use our imaginations fully. The look we aimed for is somewhere that you believe people actually lived and worked."[1]

Creating a Divided World

At the visual heart of *Shakespeare in Love* are contrasting worlds—Queen Elizabeth and the aristocracy on one side, Shakespeare and commoners on the other. Designer Childs created these worlds through a combination of original sets and modified locations. Although all of the film's action takes place in and around London, two buildings, The Rose Theatre and the De Lessep mansion, serve as production design centerpieces.

The two buildings could not be more different in appearance and significance. When the story starts, The Rose has been closed for some time due to a plague quarantine and looks abandoned and neglected. Made of coarse, unfinished wood, the structure is bare and unadorned. It is also open and round, soaring and welcoming.

Childs said, "A lot of the feel comes from the fact that there is no roof and that links it with the earth and sky. I was very keen to make it look as though the weather had got to it as they would not have been constantly repainting it. We also kept the Rose Theatre quite undecorated, but with a little bit of grandeur on the stage."[2] The open-air Rose is the "people's theater," one that commoners could attend and, as Childs points out, is earthy and natural.

By contrast, Viola's mansion, the real Broughton Castle in the Oxfordshire countryside, consists of a sprawling series of stone rectangles, perched on the edge of a river bank. When Shakespeare first appears there in pursuit of Viola, he is dominated by the massive structure. Visually, he seems to be in over his head. Later, however, Shakespeare takes advantage of the mansion's largeness to hide and blend in.

Childs stresses the differences between the two worlds in other sets as well. Shakespeare, the struggling writer, is connected visually to the Rose through his modest London home. Like that theater, his tiny quarters are rough and plain, almost squalid.

Keeping Up With the Camera

For Childs and director John Madden, bringing everyday London alive for the audience was key to making the story accessible. Many scenes in the film take place in the London streets, occurring against the backdrop of bustling activity. Since very few buildings from the Elizabethan period survive, the street sets, based on models that Childs and Madden concocted during pre-production, were built from scratch by Childs' crew.

Throughout the film's many street scenes, the camera moves to follow the characters. Consistently, Childs and set decorator Jill Quertier fill the foreground and background of these moving shots with objects and set pieces. Columns of buildings frequently appear in front of the characters as they walk or run through the crowded streets. In the background, people (extras) and objects—including carts, clotheslines, animals, and burning torches—move. The movement, often going counter to the direction of the main actor, not only gives the setting a realistic feel, but is visually stimulating as well.

Costumes and Make-up

In a press interview, costume designer Sandy Powell described an overall approach to the story that was similar to Childs' approach: "My aim was not to create absolutely historically accurate costumes, but to use a bit of artistic license and as the script is so fresh and light I felt there was room for the imagination, whilst always keeping it convincing."[3]

Powell's design of Shakespeare's costume exemplifies her approach. In all but a few scenes, Shakespeare wears the same outfit—bluish-green leather vest, white shirt, blue-green velvet pants, and high leather boots. Powell puts enough color into Shakespeare's costume to suggest his artistic nature, contrasting it with the uniformly brown and black clothes of the "money men" who follow him around. Compared to rival Lord Wessex, who dresses in many elaborate outfits, however, Shakespeare's look is simple and manly.

Powell says, "It did not help at all for me to think of this character as William Shakespeare, the great playwright. In a sense the whole film humanizes this great figure and so I wanted to design a costume that makes Joe [Fiennes] look good and makes him entirely convincing as a romantic lead."[4]

Shakespeare's hair and make-up are similarly basic. Make-up designer Lisa Westcott notes, "I obviously didn't want him to look like the classic Shakespeare image with the little forky beard and boy hair. The Will of the film is a young lad who chops his own hair, he's a struggling playwright, living a pretty hard life."[5]

Viola's costumes and make-up presented the designers with a special challenge—how to make Paltrow convincing as both an enticing young woman and a serious young man. Powell chose golds and pastels for most of Viola's costumes, while putting "Thomas Kent" in a saturated blue and purple outfit.

To emphasize Viola's role as Shakespeare's shining muse, Powell contrasts her lightly colored, unadorned gowns with the heavy, darker clothes of the surrounding aristocracy. Fiancé Sir Wessex's outfits are actually frillier and more ornate than Viola's. For Viola's Thomas Kent make-up, Westcott and fellow make-up designer Veronica Brebner kept things simple—a wig of cropped hair and a thin moustache and goatee.

In sharp contrast to Viola and Will, the character of Queen Elizabeth required an extreme approach. Elizabeth was one of the most powerful monarchs in European history, and her clothing reflected her prestige and influence. According to Powell, "Queen Elizabeth apparently had over a thousand dresses—all hugely flamboyant and over-the-top—she basically carried all her wealth on her frocks, so they were literally piled high with jewels."[6] As designed by Powell, Elizabeth's heavy, stiff dresses and lavish jewelry are as intimidating and forceful as her sharp tongue and iron will.

Elizabeth's hair and make-up were equally intense. Westcott notes that as "the Queen is quite old in the film she would have terrible skin—probably from mercury poisoning—so it was covered in make-up and her hair was undoubtedly falling out, so she always wore a wig. Apparently she had over 80 wigs, all different colors and her hairline would have receded from the front, giving her that rather severe look."[7] Despite her age at the time of the story, 60, Elizabeth was a big trend-setter—ladies of the court dutifully copied her appearance, no matter how outra-geous. Consequently, Elizabeth's "look" is echoed in the costumes and make-up of the women around her.

SEABISCUIT

Laura Hillenbrand's book *Seabiscuit: An American Legend* became a surprise bestseller in 2001. The story of three men who together turn an undersized racehorse into one of thoroughbred racing's all-time

Judi Dench portrays the powerful Queen Elizabeth in Shakespeare in Love. Like her magnificent gowns, her wigs were also heavily bejeweled.

winners, attracted Oscar-nominated writer-director Gary Ross. "What I discovered in the story [were] three characters, all broken, that could have quit. Instead they reached out to each other and formed a unique nuclear family," he says.[8] The 2003 film received Academy Award nominations for its screenplay, costume design, art direction, cinematography, editing, and sound.

The Story

In 1903, Charles Howard (Jeff Bridges) opens a bicycle repair shop in San Francisco and later becomes a successful auto dealer. After his young son dies in an automobile accident, Howard's marriage falls apart, and he is left wealthy but broken-hearted.

Cowboy Tom Smith (Chris Cooper) discovers that the open range is being fenced in and his profession has become almost obsolete.

John "Red" Pollard's (Tobey Maguire) book-loving middle-class family loses everything in the 1929 stock market crash. While he is still a teenager, Red's family abandons him. He earns a meager living working in stables and fighting in amateur boxing matches.

Howard's second wife, young actress Marcela Zabala (Elizabeth Banks), encourages him to buy a race horse. Howard hires Tom Smith, whose quiet approach to horses attracts him, as a trainer.

Smith spots something in a beaten down, undersized descendent of the great racehorse Man-O-War and persuades the Howards to acquire him. He then takes on Red as the horse's jockey.

After much work, Smith and Red turn Seabiscuit from an unruly horse into a record breaker. When Seabiscuit's achievements are belittled by the East Coast racing establishment, Howard challenges the owners of racing's Triple Crown winner, War Admiral, to a match race. Seabiscuit's underdog status appeals to ordinary people, who follow the race in large numbers.

Red is seriously injured before the race. At his insistence, fellow jockey George Woolf (Gary Stevens)

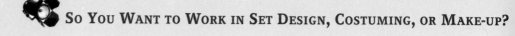

takes his place. Red listens from his hospital bed as Woolf rides Seabiscuit to victory.

Production Design

"A pencil has two ends—the lead and the eraser,'" jokes Oscar-nominated production designer Jeannine Oppewall. "On a period movie, you spend more money on the eraser to take away the present. You have to take away much of the present before you can think about putting in the past."[9]

Jeff Bridges as Charles Howard and one of the horses that played Seabiscuit in the 2003 film.

Because it is less expensive to alter existing locations than build new ones, Oppewall used her eraser often to accommodate *Seabiscuit*'s relatively small budget.

For locations that no longer existed, location scouts searched out settings, like the buildings transformed into Howard's auto dealership, that could be altered to meet the film's needs.

Oppewall found few photographs of Tijuana in the 1930s, so she based the look of the Mexican racetrack on old postcards from flea markets.

Although one major location, the Santa Anita Racetrack, still looks essentially as it did in the 1930s, some features had changed over the years. Oppewall's crew replaced awnings and other architectural features that had been removed, and tote boards and modern signage were altered. Other modern elements were digitally eliminated in post-production.

Newsreel footage and black-and-white photographs from the 1930s were mixed with new scenes shot for the movie. In order to blend the two, Oppewall had to create identical styles and locations.

For Charles Howard's estate, however, Oppewall got to use the lead end of her pencil. Rather than simply copy the original building, she took into consideration the kind of home modern viewers would expect a wealthy man to own.

> It had more to do with what I felt was appropriate
> for the character in light of what the director had
> in mind. If you go back to a lot of these old original
> California ranch houses, they're actually a lot

> smaller than what you saw in *Seabiscuit* . . . It's a sense of scale. . . .You're forced to deal with . . . growing expectations and the growing size of everything.[10]

The house's larger scale also gave the cinematographer enough room to move the camera effectively.

Racetrack announcer "Tick Tock" McGlaughlin (William Macy) was invented for the movie, so Oppewall and her crew were equally inventive in dressing his Clocker's Corner hangout, which she describes as "kinky and stinky."[11] Chock full of noise makers, musical instruments, toys, trophies, hula dolls, and girlie calendars, among many other things, it perfectly reflects Tick Tock's wild and crazy personality.

Props wordlessly tell the story of Howard's son's death. Viewers watch the boy pick up fishing rods, tackle, and other implements. Later, the same objects are shown floating in the river. Without witnessing the car crash that kills him, viewers know exactly what has occurred.

According to Oppewall, the film's overall color scheme was derived from the racing world. "There are only a few colors in *Seabiscuit*—the colors of the horses, many different beautiful shades of brown, and the colors of nature, essentially greens and cream details."[12]

In the race scenes, the track's vivid green grass and bright silks worn by the jockeys add color and excitement to the picture. The brightness of these scenes conveys the excitement Seabiscuit's career brought to ordinary people during the bleak Depression years.

Costumes

The Depression and its effect on the characters and the country is a big part of the film's story. Class differences and changes in the characters' status are brought out through the costumes.

In the 1930s, thoroughbred racing was a pursuit for wealthy owners and spectators who were not generally affected by the Depression. Makovsky wanted Californians Charles and Marcela Howard to look wealthy but informal, in keeping with their western lifestyle.

Charles Howard wears variations of a single-breasted, three-piece suit. At home and with the horses, Howard wears western-themed clothing.

Marcela evolves during the film from an eccentric, colorful dresser (reflecting her youthful, artistic personality) into a tasteful, stylish woman.

The Howard's casual, West Coast style is contrasted with that of the more conservative, old money, East Coast establishment during the challenge match race between Seabiscuit and War Admiral. Makovsky put Howard in light-colored, relaxed suits, framing his face with a white or light-colored shirt collar, while War Admiral's backers wear dark, severely-cut, pinstriped suits.

Unlike his wealthy employers, Tom Smith wears low-key functional clothing. First seen in the durable clothes of a working cowboy, after he starts training Seabiscuit, he dresses in a wool plaid jacket and fedora hat. When Seabiscuit begins winning regularly,

RESEARCH

Part of the appeal of working on a period film comes from the research that is required to reproduce a particular era. Research and observation are important because even the smallest feature lends the film authenticity.

Research begins before the job starts, says Jacqueline West, who designed the costumes for *The New World* (2005). "As soon as I learned that I would be meeting with [director Terrence Malick], I started doing research and drawings. So when I went to the meeting, I put some sketches and vivid references down on the table for him for the Native costumes."[13]

Most designers love to immerse themselves in the era they are designing for, spending weeks in archives and libraries, studying period blueprints, photographs, and paintings. Designers sometimes visit historical locations to get a feel for the setting, even when the actual spot has changed over time or will not be used for shooting.

Some directors and designers demand historical accuracy, no matter the expense or trouble. When designing and executing the Depression-era sets and costumes for the 2005 *King Kong*, Grant Major, Terry Ryan, and their large crews went to great lengths to recreate exactly details of the period. The bi-planes that shoot down Kong at the end, for example, were not only built based on period blueprints, but also included some actual vintage gauges in the instrument panels.

For most directors and designers, however, historical accuracy is a matter of relative importance. Designers will often forgo accuracy if inaccuracy suits the story better, or if duplicating a detail will prove too costly or time-consuming. For *Shakespeare in Love*, costume designer Sandy Powell chose to dress the actors appearing in *Romeo and Juliet* in costumes representative of the play's period, not in clothes contemporary to Shakespeare's time, as would have been historically accurate. "They would have worn contemporary clothes donated by rich members of society," Powell observes. "But we put them in period costumes just to show that they were putting on a play."[14]

Sometimes research has unexpected results. For *Cinderella Man*, set in New York during the Depression, costume designer Daniel Orlandi studied photos taken at that time. To his surprise, most of the people in the photos maintained an elegant appearance even when they had no money. Orlandi says: "I think our immediate impression of the Depression is usually something out of *Grapes of Wrath*, but it was actually very different in New York City. . . . It seems everyone still put on their suits on even though they didn't have any money or even if they lived on the street."[15]

Smith exchanges his working-man clothes for subdued suits.

At home, before the stock market crash, Red Pollard is dressed like any middle-class boy of the time in earth-toned trousers, shirt, and sweater vest. Later, his shabby, faded clothes reveal his penniless state.

After he is hired by Smith, Pollard appears either in a battered leather jacket and wool cap or in his jockey's silks. Although the jacket looks original to the time, it was made to order for the film and painted to look older.

Makovsky spent a lot of time studying photographs and other silks from the period to recreate the red-and-white Howard silks. "The Howard red is copied from the originals. . . . Gary Ross and [cinematographer] John Schwartzman were so great, sitting with me while we tested several pieces of red fabric to get exactly the right one on camera," Makovsky says.[16]

To accurately recreate the men's suits, she insisted on using the same kind of heavy wool that was used during the period. "The modern stuff does not compare. [The right fabric] makes these people walk differently, move differently, and live in their characters."[17]

In addition to the lead characters, Makovsky and her crew dressed more than 650 extras. For most of these, they rented costumes from all over the United States, England, and Italy. Some vintage articles were used, especially women's hats, but the fragility of the old items limited their use.

Tobey Maguire as Red Pollard in Seabiscuit.

Make-up and Hair

Make-up department head Thomas Nellen's greatest challenge was to show the characters aging over forty years without specifying their exact ages. To accomplish this, he used subtle aging techniques. Rather than create appliances for the lead characters, for example, Nellen used washes to indicate the passage of time, and he made the actors' hair progressively thinner and grayer.

At the beginning of the film, when Howard is in his twenties, he sports a full head of wild, brown

WASH—Thinned down make-up tints used for various purposes.

hair. Later, as a successful car dealer, his hair is neatly slicked back. Over the course of the film his hair and eyebrows gradually become grayer. To portray the older Howard, Bridges gained weight, and his hands and face were painted with a few age spots.

Without the use of appliances and elaborate make-up, Nellen tried to make the actors' faces resemble their real-life counterparts. To replicate Tom Smith's protruding lower lip, for instance, Chris Cooper placed a small piece of make-up sponge under his lip.

Tobey Maguire slimmed way down to accurately reproduce Red Pollard's half-starved appearance. His hair was dyed red to match the real Pollard's coloring. For Pollard's fight scenes, Nellen's crew applied blood, swellings, and cuts.

Nellen used make-up to show the effects of poverty on Pollard's family. For example, in the scenes that take place after the family loses its money, he used less make-up on actress Annie Corley (Mrs. Pollard) so that she would look gaunt and pale for the camera.

"I had to do a lot of research to find out what make-up would look like in that period, what the circumstances of people were during the Depression, and how that would be reflected in their make-up," Nellen said in an interview.[18]

PUTTING IT ALL TOGETHER:
SCIENCE FICTION, HORROR, AND FANTASY FILMS

Although production, costume, and make-up designers invariably work in a variety of genres during their careers, no genres offer them as many opportunities to explore and invent as science fiction, horror, and fantasy.

Arguably, the first science fiction-fantasy film was Georges Méliès' 1902 short *The Trip to the Moon*. Using painted backdrops and simple animation techniques, Méliès imagined the moon as a human face (the man in the moon) dotted with fantastic mushrooms and insect-like aliens. His vision was more fanciful than realistic, but showed film's potential for creating whole new vistas.

The 1927 German silent *Metropolis*, directed by Fritz Lang, is generally considered the first notable science fiction feature. Set in 2026, in a city-state divided literally by class, the film was unlike anything previously put on screen. The production design, inspired by the skyscrapers of New York but with an expressionist twist, startled contemporary audiences and inspired many filmmakers of later generations. The robot costume worn by the lead actress, which was made out of a revolutionary plastic wood, is still considered a marvel of movie costuming.

EXPRESSIONISM— A style of filmmaking that distorts time and space and emphasizes basic qualities of people and objects.

Hollywood's *Frankenstein* (1931), directed by James Whale, blended science fiction and horror and introduced American audiences to the now-classic mad scientist's laboratory set. Tod Browning's *Dracula* (1931) created an image of vampires that still resonates today. Art director Charles D. Hall and make-up man Jack P. Pierce worked on both films and contributed to many more pictures in the genres.

Pure fantasy movies have also been around since the beginning; many early silent films were adaptations of such fairy tales as *Cinderella* and *Snow White*. With its remarkable use of color, the art direction behind *The Wizard of Oz* (1939) brought new complexity to live-action fantasy films.

In 1968, the modern generation of science-fiction and fantasy design was ushered in by Stanley Kubrick's *2001: A Space Odyssey*. Kubrick's sophisticated and beautiful rendering of the future helped give science-fiction films a respectability they still enjoy today. Other influential late twentieth-century science-fiction movies included George Miller's *Mad Max* trilogy, Ridley Scott's *Blade Runner* (1982), and George Lucas' *Star Wars* movies, in which life on other worlds was imagined in near-mythic detail.

With the release of *Superman* in 1978, the late twentieth century also saw the birth of the live-action superhero fantasy film. Unlike previous superhero movies and TV shows, *Superman* employed top-notch production, costume, and make-up designers, including *Star Wars* veterans John Barry and Stuart Freeborn. *Batman* (1989) and its sequels and *Dick Tracy* (1990) brought even more complexity to the lavish fantasy trend.

Today, with the advance of computer-generated imaging and digital technology, science fiction, fantasy, and horror films are more popular than ever. No summer or holiday movie season would be complete without a big-budget fantasy adventure or superhero epic.

BLADE RUNNER

Released in 1982, *Blade Runner* became an instant cult favorite, earning a permanent place in the pantheon of science fiction films. The psychologically rich story proved groundbreaking for the science fiction genre. The film also provided artistically trained director Ridley Scott, who had scored a success with another science fiction classic, *Alien* (1979), a perfect outlet for visual invention.

In addition to Scott's direction, key to the movie's triumph was production designer Lawrence K. Paull's Oscar-nominated depiction of futuristic Los Angeles, and the striking costumes and make-up and hair of Michael Kaplan, Charles Knode, Marvin G. and Michael Westmore, and Shirley Padgett.

Many critics have compared the dark urban feel of *Blade Runner* to detective movies of the 1940s and 1950s, collectively referred to as *film noir* (black or dark film). Visually, film noir movies are characterized by shadows, rain, oblique and vertical lines, and harsh geometric shapes.

The Story

Based loosely on Philip K. Dick's 1968 novel *Do Androids Dream of Electric Sheep?*, *Blade Runner* is a detective story set in 2019. By that time, other planets, collectively called "Off-world," have been colonized with the help of slave Replicants, human clones with super strength and intelligence. Because some of the androids have become violently independent, all Replicants have been outlawed on Earth, and police detectives known as blade runners have been hunting and terminating them when needed.

After four especially dangerous Replicants find their way to Los Angeles, where their brilliant but cold corporate maker Eldon Tyrell (Joe Turkel) resides, newly retired blade runner Rick Deckard (Harrison Ford) reluctantly agrees to track them down. While hunting the Replicant fugitives, led by the charismatic Roy Batty (Rutger Hauer), Deckard meets beautiful, mysterious Rachael (Sean Young), Tyrell's newest android invention.

Rachael, who is unaware she is a Replicant, challenges Deckard's notion of what makes a human being human, especially after she saves his life by shooting one of the fugitives. She also causes him to question the correctness of his mission, which includes orders to terminate her.

Architecture—East Meets West

When he first began work on *Blade Runner,* director Ridley Scott envisioned the story's setting as a hybrid of New York and Tokyo, the West and the East. Specifically, Scott wanted to create a world that was set forty years in the future, but had the look and feel of a place forty years in the past. Scott's vision was atypical of most science fiction movies of the day, which tended to present the future as either wholly new and ultra-modern or barren and primeval.

Constructing the future world of *Blade Runner* required a combination of design techniques. Filming on location in New York was not feasible, so Warner Bros.' "Old New York" backlot, a recreation of early twentieth century Manhattan, served as the story's primary street set. Los Angeles eventually became the story's locale, and shots depicting the Los Angeles skyline and other long views of the city were created using miniatures and other special effects supplied by Douglas Trumbull and Richard Yuricich. Actual Los

63

Angeles locations, such as Union Station, the downtown Bradbury Building, and architect Frank Lloyd Wright's hilltop Ennis-Brown house, were also utilized.

Working closely with Scott, designer Paull and "futurist" Syd Mead topped the old-fashioned brick-and-mortar New York set with neon signs and rows of metal pipes and tubes. Familiar European and American design elements were blended with more exotic Asian elements. In this future urban landscape, distinctions between cultures melted away, leaving a crowded mash-up of periods and styles.

For inspiration, Paull "brought in just about my entire architectural research library, and we went from Egyptian to Deco to Streamline Moderne to Classical, from [architects] Frank Lloyd Wright to Antonio Gaudí. We turned the photographs sideways, upside down, inside out, and backwards to stretch where we were going and came up with a street that looked like *Conan the Barbarian* in 2020. . . . [I]t had to be richly carved. I didn't want right angles; I didn't want slick surfaces."[1] Appropriately Fritz Lang's *Metropolis* also provided architectural inspiration.

Home, Sweet Home

Though trained as a city planner, Paull never conceived the *Blade Runner* metropolis as an abstract whole. Instead, he focused on how the specific locations mentioned in the script would reflect the daily lives of the characters. Paull noted that few visual details were found in the screenplay but that the script provided him with an emotional and thematic foundation for his design. He knew, for example, that in addition to the city being a hodge-podge of styles, it would appear uniformly rundown and polluted:

"You go back to the script, and the middle classes have the left the earth . . . who's left in the center of the city but the working class, the unemployed, the homeless. These people do not have the wherewithal, the education, the skills to fix what breaks in the city. Therefore, when things like heating and air conditioning break down within buildings, they can't go internally and fix it."[2]

Once Paull seized on the idea of a gerry rigged infrastructure, he included retrofitting, or adding new or modified parts to existing structures or devices, to many of the sets. *Blade Runner* sets bulge with odd parts and pieces that add to the visual density of every scene. Virtually every setting employs deep perspective, and telling details fill every nook and cranny of the frame. Set decorator Linda DeScenna and her crew went to great lengths to create props and decorations—from elaborate store signage down to magazine covers at a newsstand and warning labels on the parking meters—that complete Scott's film noir future world.

Space in *Blade Runner* fluctuates between the claustrophobia of the street, where "spinners"—flying police cars designed by Mead—and motorized billboards hover oppressively overhead, to the palatial vastness of Tyrell's penthouse home. In keeping with his wealthy station, Tyrell's home, with its high ceilings and large rectangular rooms, is elegantly furnished. Despite its beauty, Tyrell's penthouse has a museum-like quality that keeps its occupants at arm's length.

The home of Tyrell's eccentric genetic designer Sebastian (William Sanderson) is also vast, but unlike Tyrell's penthouse, Sebastian's space, an entire downtown building, is decrepit. Packed randomly into the interior of his apartment proper are his eccentric, animated inventions, scientific gadgets, games, and toys. An electric beaker has been jury-rigged to serve as an egg boiler. In the outside hallway, rain leaks through the ceilings and searchlights penetrate broken windows. A feeling of loneliness and gloom permeates the structure. Fittingly, the building becomes the setting of Deckard and Batty's final confrontation.

By contrast, Deckard's apartment, according to Paull, was designed to be cavelike. "It was his womb, so the rooms were very linear, very overbearing, and the walls bracketed out like a series of contemporary vaults."[3] In keeping with the cave idea (and film noir style), shadows dominate. The viewer only glimpses nooks and crannies, never the whole space. Deckard's belongings reflect his divided emotional state, a mix of old and new. In one area sits a piano covered with black-and-white family photographs—the past, real and imagined. In another are Deckard's electronic tools-of-the-trade, high-tech machines for analyzing images.

Color—Hot and Cold

In the opening aerial shot of *Blade Runner*, Los Angeles appears as a blanket of golden lights, punctuated by massive smoke stacks that belch explosive reddish fire above the skyline. Down below, at street level, all is wet and bluish, except for the occasional roaring trashcan fire. For the film's exteriors Paull "used many warm gray tones and a great deal of natural aging, dust and everything. The only time we saw hot color was in the neon at night."[4] Blue is also the color of the searchlights that constantly probe the lower half of the city.

In contrast to the cool colors of the street, Tyrell's soaring penthouse is bathed in sunlight. At night, it is lit with scores of flaming candelabras. Candles are also used to illuminate the upscale nightclub where Deckard tracks down one of the Replicants. In general, the more exclusive parts of the city enjoy the brightest and warmest atmosphere.

Texture—And the Rains Came Down

One of the most notable aspects of the *Blade Runner* design is its rain. From the beginning, Scott included rain as an important dramatic element in the story. Although the story takes place in November—the start of Los Angeles' rainy season—the constant drenching that takes place suggests a world out of synch. Earth has become an undesirable place in which to live, coated with pollutants like acid rain.

Blade Runner's nighttime rain adds texture and movement to the sets—in many shots, streams of water are seen cascading down walls and bouncing off set pieces. The rain also comments on the bleakness of the setting and the poignancy of the Replicants' desire to live at any cost, even in a world half-destroyed by the very humans who are determined to kill them.

Costumes

As with the film's production design, Charles Knode and William Kaplan's costumes reflect Ridley Scott's premise that in any not-too-distant future, styles will look both old and new. In the case of *Blade Runner,* the costumes are a mix of retro 1940s, 1980s punk, Asian peasant, and futuristic twenty-first century. "A contemporary man wouldn't be puzzled," according to Scott, "by forties clothing . . . Fashion is always cyclical."[5]

The film's costumes, like the production design, mirror the class structure of the depicted society. In one scene wealthy Tyrell wears a suit with an elaborate bowtie and in another a luxurious, padded dressing gown. Other well-to-do types are garbed in feathers and furs, ostentatious adornments in a society in which animals such as snakes and owls have become all but extinct.

On the other end of the class spectrum are the food vendors and roving street people. According to Paull, "Charles found most of the clothes for the actors and extras in used clothing stores. . . . It was literally, 'Put it in the washing machine, pour a pound of real strong coffee in, and see what happens.' That's basically it; everything was very browned over, very heavily aged and crusted over."[6]

In addition to their economic status, the film's costumes help define the characters' occupations as well as their personalities. During much of the movie, Deckard, for example, wears a trench coat. Long associated with detectives, particularly 1940s film noir detectives, the trench coat reminds the audience that Deckard is a professional on a mission. His earth-toned patterned shirts and ties, however, hint at the man underneath—complex, subtle, warm.

Similarly, the ethnicity and attitude of Deckard's police partner Gaff (Edward James Olmos) is represented by Gaff's modified zoot suit, attire invented in the 1940s by rebellious African Americans and Latinos. Although assigned to keep Deckard on track with his mission, Gaff ultimately helps the blade runner flee. Gaff's distinctive costume immediately paints him as an outsider capable of breaking the rules.

Costumes worn by the Replicants underscore their conflicted emotional and professional life. During most of the movie, Batty, the group's blond, blue-eyed leader, wears a long leather coat reminiscent of a Nazi SS officer. Underneath, however, are pants and undershirt suggestive of a futuristic prison uniform. As represented in his clothing, Batty is both a dangerous military type and a captive of fate. Replicant Leon (Brion James), who at first poses as a Tyrell Corporation waste management engineer, is appropriately nondescript in his work uniform. Later on the street, however, he appears in a leather coat that links him visually to Batty.

The female Replicant costumes also reflect the characters' dual nature. "Combat model" Zhora (Joanna Cassidy) has disguised herself as an exotic snake dancer whose street clothes are sexy and revealing but hard as nails. As Deckard pursues and terminates her, however, her see-through plastic raincoat reveals not her feminine strength but her human vulnerability.

Young Pris (Darryl Hannah), a Replicant "pleasure model," is decked out in clothes that are a cross between punk and streetwalker. Though she is Batty's lover, he commands her to seduce Sebastian in order to gain access to Tyrell. Despite her rebellious tendencies, Pris remains in the grip of men until the very end, as her clothes and make-up imply.

When first seen, Rachael is wearing a shiny black 1940s business suit with broad padded shoulders and narrow waist. The severe tailored look suggests both her seriousness and her specialness. Black hints at the danger and sadness surrounding the one-of-a-kind Replicant. As she spends more time with Deckard, however, her clothes, including a full-length fur coat, soften in style, color, and material.

Make-up and Hair

Not surprisingly, make-up and hair in *Blade Runner* coordinate appropriately with the costumes and production design. Marvin G. Westmore, who hails from a long line of legendary movie make-up artists going back to the silent period, acted as chief make-up

Rutger Hauer portrays the Replicant leader Roy Batty in Blade Runner. *His bleach blond hair and long leather coat convey his status as a dangerous and fearless outlaw.*

artist, executing special effects, beauty, and straight make-up techniques.

Westmore described his make-up assignment on the movie this way: "One day I might have to apply a beauty make-up to Sean Young, whose look was definitely patterned after the glamour queens of the 1940s. . . . I kept Sean's make-up exceedingly simple. Foundation, blusher, eyeliner. That was it."[7] On the other extreme was the make-up for Sebastian. Tyrell's young designer suffers from a glandular disease that causes premature aging. To make Sebastian look young and old at the same time, Westmore used the classic make-up technique "stretch and stipple."

Westmore also employed a special aging make-up technique called "Rembrandt" (after the seventeenth-century painter) for the Replicants, whose pre-programmed death is fast approaching when the story starts. Westmore's aging of the Replicants subtly reminds the audience that these otherwise strong and healthy clones are involved in a life-and-death crisis.

To match the characters' 1940s clothing, hairstylist Shirley Padgett, whose previous credits included the *Wonder Woman* TV series, gave the women pompadours, hairdos popular during that decade. Rachael's tightly rolled hair helps convey to the viewer her controlled, manufactured perfection. During a love scene with Deckard, Rachael lets down her long, thick hair, symbolically implying not only her loss of control but her growing humanity as well.

Special effects prosthetic make-up was supplied by the veteran John Chambers and Marvin's brother, the uncredited Michael Westmore, who later made a name for himself working on various *Star Trek* television shows. Prosthetics make-up was used most often in the fight scenes, especially in the final showdown between Deckard and Batty. Among other tricks Chambers and Westmore fashioned a fake head for Tyrell, fake broken fingers for Deckard, and a fake hand with a nail through it for Batty.

THE CHRONICLES OF NARNIA: THE LION, THE WITCH AND THE WARDROBE

Based on the popular children's book by British author C. S. Lewis, *The Chronicles of Narnia: The Lion, the Witch and the Wardrobe* creates two very different worlds: historical England during World War II, and the magical realm of Narnia.

Lewis has said that his inspiration for the book was an image of "a faun carrying an umbrella in the snow," but he wrote very few descriptions of his characters.[8] Director Andrew Adamson (*Shrek* and *Shrek 2*), however, had read the Narnia books as a child and had definite ideas of how the sets, costumes, and make-up should look.

Adamson collaborated with Oscar-winning production designer Roger Ford, costume designer Isis Mussenden, special effects make-up artists Howard Berger and Gregory Nicotero, and make-up designer

Nikki Gooley and their crews to make each world seem real and believable.

The Story

The four Pevensie children, Peter (William Moseley), the eldest, Susan (Anna Popplewell), Edmund (Skandar Keynes), and the youngest, Lucy (Georgie Henley), are sent by their mother from London to the safer countryside home of Professor Kirke.

During a game of hide-and-seek, Lucy discovers an old wardrobe in an unused spare room. Through it, she enters Narnia, a land ruled by Jadis, the White Witch (Tilda Swinton), where it is "always winter but never Christmas."

By a lamppost, Lucy meets the faun Mr. Tumnus, who invites her to tea, intending to turn her over to the Witch. He has second thoughts, however, and helps her return to the wardrobe.

Lucy comes back to Narnia with her sister and brothers. There, Mr. and Mrs. Beaver reveal a prophesy that human children will help return the lion king Aslan to power. Edmund is lured by the Witch's false promises into temporarily betraying his siblings and their Narnian allies. As Aslan's forces unite and the Witch's power weakens, spring comes to Narnia. The Witch claims the right to kill her escaped prisoner, Edmund, but agrees to spare him if Aslan will take his place. Aslan's death is only temporary, however. He returns to life and rouses Peter's army to victory.

The Pevensie children enter a magical and dangerous world in The Chronicles of Narnia: The Lion, the Witch and the Wardrobe *(2005). From left to right: Lucy Pevensie (Georgie Henley), Susan Pevensie (Anna Popplewell), Peter Pevensie (William Moseley), and Edmund Pevensie (Skandar Keynes).*

Production Design
London

"We tried to build up a believable England before we moved into Narnia," says Roger Ford.[9] Brief scenes of a nighttime bombing raid introduce the Pevensie children and their conflicts. The scenes also ground the magical world of Narnia in a grim reality, drawing a parallel between war in the real world and the war the children will help fight in Narnia.

Andrew Adamson suggested different palettes for each important sequence in the film: muted grays for the bombing scenes, icy blue and white for wintry Narnia, and an explosion of golds and greens when Aslan returns.

Professor Kirke's House

The warm reds, pinks, and wood tones in Professor Kirke's house create a feeling of safety and refuge. Yet, its many rooms and confusing passages mirror the disorienting events the children have experienced. For Peter, who as the eldest is responsible for his siblings, things are more complicated. In one scene, he gazes out through a leaded glass window resembling prison bars, which emphasizes his feelings of isolation and powerlessness.

The woodwork and shape of the room containing the magical wardrobe are designed to draw viewers' eyes to it. The gauzy material covering the wardrobe floats slowly to the ground when Lucy tugs at it, hinting at the important adventure to come.

A Parallel World

For Narnia "Andrew didn't want a fantasy world, but a parallel world that would relate to our own," Roger Ford explains.[10] Although magical, Narnia duplicates many real-world elements.

For example, everything in the Beavers' home is built to beaver scale, including miniature tools, fishing rods, textiles, and homemade preserves. The interior was constructed from sticks of various sizes made to look as if they had been gnawed by the beavers. The beaver theme even extends to the chips (French fries) Mrs. Beaver offers her guests—a plate of actual wood chips. A frozen flow of water was included when research showed that real beaver dams have water flowing through them.

At first, Beaver Lodge's tiny size seems cozy, but its size has additional implications. Children in hiding, as the Pevensies are, instinctively conceal themselves in small spaces. And their discomfort as they cramp their bodies onto the Beavers' small chairs represents their unreadiness to accept their true places in Narnia.

> EDWARDIAN—The period from 1901 to 1910 that coincides with the reign of King Edward VII in the United Kingdom. At this time, rapid industrialization resulted in more social mobility. Clothing was looser and more flexible than during the rigid Victorian era that preceded it.

The lamppost that lights the children's way in and out of Narnia is another blending of historical England with magical Narnia. Ford added a gnarled metal structure to the bottom of a replica of an Edwardian lamppost, making it look as if it had grown roots.

Winter versus Spring

The White Witch and Aslan represent the two opposing forces in Narnia. The Witch's Narnia is frozen in perpetual winter, so everything in her world seems to be made of ice and snow. The design of her chariot and throne, for example, was inspired by photographs of crystalline snowflakes.

Although her castle is not described that way in the book, "we made a very rash decision early on that we would make our castle out of ice," Ford says. "That all seemed very exciting at the time, but then, of course, came the problem for me of how to build a castle out of ice."[11]

After some experimentation, Ford used fiberglass with a bit of blue coloring mixed in. Fluorescent lighting and blue gels lend the castle a properly icy look, and to enhance the illusion, sounds of cracking ice play on the sound track.

Aslan, on the other hand, is associated with golden colors and the sun. As his power ascends, ice melts on the ground, trees blossom, and gold dominates the color scheme. Prior to shooting, Ford fertilized the grass at the New Zealand location where Aslan's camp would be built, so it would be as green as possible.

For Cair Paravel, where the children are crowned kings and queens of Narnia, Ford deviated from the medieval castle illustrated in the book. "I thought, we're in Narnia after all . . . It is its own world . . . We started to think of Cair Paravel as a light-filled palace of celebration and joy," he says.[12] Its vast spaces are awe-inspiring, as befits the children's new royal status.

Costumes

The Pevensie Children

Costume designer Isis Mussenden's biggest challenge was "dressing the children because they were always growing. Any given dress had to be made 12 times."[13]

Throughout the film, the children wear wools in blues and earth tones, subdued colors and textures that underscore the seriousness of their task. Lucy, however, is often in shades of red or pink, which establish her central role in the story.

By contrast, the children's coronation garments are made from rich velvets and shiny satins in Aslan's colors of gold, green, and silver.

Even though armored helmets have a protective plate in front of the face, Ford left Peter's helmet open so viewers could see his face during the battle scenes and witness his emotions as he assumes leadership.

The White Witch

The Witch's costumes make her look as cold and unfeeling as her wintry realm. As actress Tilda Swinton says: "It's like the White Witch is made of water or ice or smoke or something natural."[14]

To create a frosty effect, Mussenden layered velvet, felted wool, shimmering silk, metallic lace, and organza. Although it seems like the Witch changes her outfit for every scene, the costumes were meant to be seen as one dress, which changes color and expands or contracts, like a supernatural plant, depending on her mood.

The White Witch (Tilda Swinton) plans to turn Edmund Pevensie (Skandar Keynes) against his siblings to prevent Aslan from recapturing the throne. Dressed from head to toe in winter white, she looks as cold and cruel on the outside as she is in the inside.

At the height of her power, the Witch wears a white dress with a huge collar, white furs, and a crown of icicles. After the children's arrival, her power fades and her dress becomes grayish. It continues to darken and narrow in silhouette as Aslan's power increases.

When the Witch kills Aslan, she should be at her most powerful, but, like a dying plant, her dress shrinks and turns black, forecasting her coming defeat. A dead

SPECIAL EFFECTS IN PRODUCTION DESIGN

If given the choice, most designers would prefer to build every inch of a set to scale, in great, realistic detail. Often, however, they end up faking at least some of their presentation. All designers must balance the dramatic needs of a scene with the physical and budgetary limitations of a production.

Today, production limitations can be compensated for through a variety of special visual effects, including digital or computer-generated imaging (CGI); blue and green screen processes, in which actors perform scenes in front of blank blue or green screens; miniatures; and matte shots, in which a painting is combined with blue or green screen process shots, or a digital image is combined with a live-action shot.

Although any type of movie can employ special effects, fantasy and science fiction films use them most often. The entire 2004 fantasy film *Sky Captain and the World of Tomorrow*, for instance, was shot using the blue screen process. In the 2005 *King Kong*, only the bottom half of the Skull Island village was real. The top half was done using miniatures. For the Empire State Building scenes, fully constructed sets were mixed with CGI images.

black rooster perches on the dress's collar, illustrating her cruel and predatory nature.

Character and Special Effects Make-up

The children's look changes very little over the course of the film. In the coronation scenes, however, Susan has longer hair, and Lucy's hair is curled. The slight difference subtly shows how much time has passed while the children have been in Narnia. Some of the other characters are much more interesting visually.

The White Witch

To emphasize the White Witch's chilly, non-human qualities, make-up artist Nikki Gooley bleached Swinton's eyebrows and added white fibers to her eyelashes. Swinton herself suggested the mass of dreadlocked hair that springs from her head as if it were alive.

Remembering the way cats' pupils enlarge when they are hunting, Adamson suggested that Swinton wear black contact lenses when she kills Aslan, for an intense, aggressive look. In the battle scenes, Gooley says: "We later gave her more color on her face, to maybe reflect the blood of Aslan."[15]

ANIMATRONIC—
A remote-controlled system that uses mechanical devices to produce a life-like performance using puppets or models.

Aslan

In most scenes, Aslan was digitally generated, but special effects make-up artist Howard Berger, who won an Academy Award for the film's make-

This minotaur-like warrior was just one of the many diverse inhabitants of Narnia.

Fantasy and Special Effects Make-up

Fantasy and special effects make-up helps give life to characters who do not exist, but who must seem real to the viewer. The make-up may include any combination of straight make-up, sculpture, latex and plastics, painting, appliances, mechanical devices, puppets, camera tricks, and digital manipulation.

For the 1986 film *Harry and the Hendersons*, special effects make-up artist Rick Baker used an animatronic mask, a mask with mechanical devices inside to form expressions, to turn Kevin Peter Hall into the ape-like Bigfoot, Harry. "If you glue a foam rubber appliance that's too thick onto an actor's face, his facial movements will be so inhibited that the character can't be expressive," Baker explains. "You have to use an animatronic mask."[16] Harry's head was set in motion by small servomotors inside the face, which were controlled by the actor and three other technicians.

Robot make-up designed by special effects designer Stan Winston and his team for *A. I. Artificial Intelligence* created the illusion of mechanical robot heads showing behind their human-appearing faces with a combination of prosthetics, beauty make-up, and computer graphics (CG). To facilitate the CG insertion of mechanical works into each robot's head, Winston incorporated a blue skull cap, which enabled visual effects artists to remove that part of the head in post-production and replace it with mechanics.[17]

up, his partner Greg Nicotero, and their crew built three animatronic versions of Narnia's lion king. One full-sized creature was made to aid the digital artists. Susan and Lucy rode another version in green screen shots.

The most memorable version, however, is the dying Aslan. The animatronic puppet contained breathing mechanisms and a radio-controlled head. "Prior to the shot, we had it up and breathing, so there would be some form of emotion, and the girls were able to touch him," Berger explains.[18]

Mr. Tumnus

James McAvoy, who plays Mr. Tumnus, a half-goat, half-human faun, was fitted with a fiberglass skullcap, silicone ears, and a radio-controlled device to make the ears wiggle. The entire apparatus was covered by a thick curly wig.

The make-up crew laid hair along the underside of McAvoy's forearms and over his chest, back, and face. To complete his make-up, McAvoy was given a gelatin nose piece that made his nose look more faun-like. McAvoy wore green pants, which were replaced in post-production with computer-generated goat's legs.

Berger and Nicotero also created 170 characters from twenty-three species. "We used every trick in the book: foam appliances, gelatin appliances, silicone pieces. We had full giant suits that were all fabricated and ventilated. There was an unbelievable amount of hair work, between wigs and facial pieces, and a lot of hand-laying, so it was an enormous task," Berger says.[19]

5

PUTTING IT ALL TOGETHER: CONTEMPORARY FILMS

Though usually less flashy than period or science fiction films, contemporary movies—those set in recent times—test the talents of designers in a variety of ways. Since realism is often the goal of contemporary stories, production designers have to find ways to make the visual world of the film credible and recognizable, while at the same time advancing the drama through such artistic elements as palette and architecture. Likewise, costume designers and make-up artists often must discover subtle ways to express character within an otherwise standard contemporary look. Movies like *Crash* and *Napoleon Dynamite* skillfully use contemporary design techniques to maintain everyday realism and create unique characters and stories.

CRASH

The 2004 film *Crash*, written by Paul Haggis and Bobby Moresco, examines racial conflict in Los Angeles by following encounters between a cross-section of residents from different classes and ethnic groups.

Writer-director Haggis' own car-jacking experience inspired the film's dark story of racial conflict. Despite its despairing tone, *Crash*'s message resonated strongly with viewers, and the controversial film won Academy Awards for Best Picture and Best Original Screenplay.

The Story

Homicide detective Graham Waters (Don Cheadle) and his partner and girlfriend Ria (Jennifer Esposito) are rear-ended by a Korean woman. Ria and the woman exchange ethnic slurs.

On the prior evening, two young African-American men, Anthony (Chris 'Ludacris' Bridges) and Peter (Larenz Tate) steal the car belonging to District Attorney Rick Cabot (Brendan Fraser) and his wife Jean (Sandra Bullock). At home, Jean accuses Daniel (Michael Peña) a Hispanic locksmith, of being a gang member.

African-American television director Cameron (Terrence Howard) and his wife Christine (Thandie Newton) are stopped by white police officers Ryan (Matt Dillon) and Hanson (Ryan Phillippe). Ryan molests Christine, which disgusts Hanson and creates a rift between Christine and Cameron.

Iranian Farhad (Shaun Toub) tries to buy a gun to protect himself. Despite the intervention of his physician daughter Dorri (Bahar Soomekh), he becomes involved in a heated argument with the store owner, who calls him "Osama." During the rest of the evening, the characters cross each other's paths in unexpected ways. Some encounters provide insights, while others, such as the shooting death of Peter, end in tragedy.

Production Design

In the film's opening, Graham expresses one of the movie's themes: "In L.A., nobody touches you. We're always behind this metal and glass." Although this line refers to the cars that prevent people from connecting, scenes are often shot through windows, doors, or in mirrors, stressing the characters' isolation.

Nominated for an Art Directors Guild award, Laurence Bennett's production design underscores the themes of separation and confinement. Many scenes take place in small spaces. At the Ryan home, for example, Ryan's ill father is framed in the door of a lighted bathroom, while Ryan stands to the side in the dark.

This illustration of Ryan's inability to connect with his father is contrasted with a pivotal moment between Daniel and his daughter, when the small space under her bed creates a warm, intimate mood.

Other scenes, like the shot of a solitary Graham, standing in the vast hall of a government building after he agrees to suppress evidence, use space to underscore feelings of alienation.

The story takes place around Christmas, traditionally a season of forgiveness and reconciliation. Perhaps to show how little importance those feelings have for the characters, holiday references are limited. The rare snowfall that ends the film, however, represents the characters' possibility of absolution.

Filmed in just thirty-five days and produced on a very small budget, the filmmakers cut corners when possible. To save time and money, Haggis used the same house for two different families. "We painted three of the walls in one room red and left one corner unpainted. The painted side became Thandie and Terrence's house, and the unpainted side became Matt Dillon's house," he explains.[1]

The Cabot house (Haggis' actual house) is one of the few sets that contain more than one room. Here, too, Bennett uses space to express disconnection, as Jean and Rick talk to each other from separate rooms, symbolizing the emotional distance between them.

Shot mainly with a palette of browns, whites, and grays, red is used throughout in both clothing and interiors to add emotional punch and to evoke an empathetic reaction from viewers.

Unlike the tasteful but conventional decor in the Cabots' home, the red walls of Christine and Cameron's bedroom are decorated with contemporary paintings and ethnic art, reflecting their personal taste. The room's warm coloring underscores the emotional confrontations between husband and wife.

Props help convey social class and income. In Graham's mother's house, for example, a piano and nicely framed photographs contrast with nearby drug paraphernalia, implying earlier, better times and explaining in shorthand what Graham is trying so hard to escape.

The inexpensive items in Farhad's cluttered store make it clear that his family is barely getting by. His efforts to survive make his explosive anger more understandable.

Daniel's home, in a lower-middle-class neighborhood, is filled with children's drawings. The handmade-looking afghans on his daughter's bed and ruffled curtains in her room point to close family ties.

Costumes and Make-up

Because *Crash* is an allegorical, ensemble film, characters are not developed in depth. "I wanted to play with stereotypes, with the assumptions we make about strangers," explains Haggis.[2] Costumes by Linda Bass; make-up by Ben Nye, Jr.; and hairstyles by Bunny Parker, Kerry Mendenhall, and Kimberley Spiteri, are used to create a snapshot of each character's ethnicity, class, and emotional state. For Linda Bass "the challenge was to capture all the different strata of the city and to make it look real. I couldn't even go through magazines, because what I was going for wouldn't be in a magazine."[3]

ALLEGORICAL—
Representing abstract ideas or principles with characters in a dramatic or narrative form such as a play, movie, or book.

In a switch from the usual situation, clothes and make-up are often intentionally deceptive. As Haggis says, "I wanted to give you a lot of characters you could judge very quickly and know very quickly—or think you knew very quickly."[4]

The Police

Graham's tailored wool suit, crisp white shirt, and tie mark him as the supervising partner. His hair is short and neat and unlike many detectives, he is clean

Farhad (Shaun Toub) and his daughter Dorri (Bahar Soomekh) argue with the owner (Jack McGee) of a gun store while an officer (Jayden Lund) holds Farhad back in Crash.

shaven. His appearance is ambitious and professional, but his clothes also reveal his insecurities.

As a black man, Graham wants everyone to take him seriously. His expensive suit, nicer than those worn by most homicide detectives, shows how strongly he wants to move up.

Ria's hair is long and loose. She wears little make-up, and her clothes, in dark shades except for the red sweater glimpsed under her jacket, are casual and inexpensive. Her leather jacket projects a toughness appropriate to her profession. According to Linda Bass, Ria is purposely dressed down to emphasize the efforts Graham makes to look flawlessly professional.[5]

Ryan's and Hanson's standard-issue uniforms are like armor, masking any personal information. Even in plain clothes, they dress in similar casual pants and plaid shirts. Their clothes reveal nothing, so their actions cannot be predicted.

The Immigrants

Two contrasting immigrant families appear in the film. The Korean woman's heavy accent reveals that she is a recent immigrant, but judging by her clothes and her car, she has done well. Her husband first appears in a trench coat, which while revealing nothing, seems vaguely sinister. Later, their wealth is revealed to come from smuggling illegal immigrants.

The Iranian family has not been as fortunate. Farhad's collarless shirt and old pullover peg him immediately as foreign. Dorri is dressed in more expensive, professional, American-style clothes. For her heated confrontation with the gun store owner, Bass dressed her in red. The mother's head scarf and long dress show her to be the least assimilated family member.

The Gangsters

At the beginning of the film, Anthony and Peter wear medium-priced, department store clothes, like college students. Despite their neat hair, respectable clothes, and proper English, the men meet with real or perceived prejudice. Viewers are forced to question their initial sympathy when the men turn out to be carjackers.

The Powerful

Judging from their clothes and the expensive Navigator they drive, District Attorney Rick Cabot and his wife Jean are very wealthy. Rick wears a standard, although beautifully tailored, dark suit. Jean's high-necked dress, covered with an enveloping, protective black cashmere wrap, indicates a frightened, ill-at-ease woman.

The crisp shirt and slacks Jean wears at home emphasize her tense, prickly nature. Her bigoted, fearful comments about blacks and Latinos are of a piece with her severe clothing. A later change in Jean's attitudes and behavior is signaled by softer sweat suits and a lower-cut tank top.

Although wealthy, Cameron and Christine are in many ways the opposite of Rick and Jean. Because of their race, their social status is less secure.

Cameron's outfits include a turtleneck cashmere sweater under a European-cut suit and a button-down shirt and roll-necked sweater. Soft edges hint at his emotional defenselessness. His hair is straightened, and he has a neatly-trimmed goatee, symbolizing his attempts to fit into the white establishment.

Cameron's well-groomed appearance is contrasted with that of his casually dressed, unshaven, white producer, (Tony Danza). Their different styles underscore the humiliation Cameron feels when he submits to the producer's authority.

Christine first appears in a glittery, sensuous, body-hugging outfit, cut low in the back. Her neatly coiffed hair and white dress characterize her as a respectable woman, despite her flirty behavior. By baring Christine's back rather than her breasts, Bass shows her as vulnerable instead of brazen.

NAPOLEON DYNAMITE

Made by first-time feature director Jared Hess on a shoestring budget of $400,000, *Napoleon Dynamite* was the sleeper hit of 2004. Between its first limited release in June 2004 to February 2005, *Napoleon Dynamite* racked up $44,541,000 in box office receipts.

Inspired by Hess' real life growing up in a small Idaho town, *Napoleon Dynamite* is the ultimate beginners film, a demonstration of how much can be done with limited resources and experience. At the time of production, very few in the crew had more than a couple of credits to their names, if that. Neophyte co-screenwriter Jerusha Hess (Hess' wife) doubled as the film's costume designer.

The Story

Misfit high schooler Napoleon Dynamite (Jon Heder) lives in rural Preston, Idaho, with his grandmother (Sandy Martin), pet llama Tina, and thirty-two-year-old brother Kip (Aaron Ruell). In school Napoleon, who fills his days drawing pictures of mythical creatures, riding his bike, and playing tether ball, is tormented by bullies and scorned by girls. At home he fights with the underachieving Kip and is ignored by his busy grandmother.

Napoleon's dull life begins to change after he meets fellow students Pedro Sanchez (Efren Ramirez), a Mexican immigrant new to town, and the socially inept Deb (Tina Majorino), an aspiring fashion photographer. The quietly optimistic Pedro inspires Napoleon to be bolder with girls, while Deb's gentle nature makes the opposite sex a little less intimidating for him. Napoleon's existence is further altered when his grandmother is hospitalized after an ATV accident and his uncle Rico (Jon Gries), who yearns to return to 1982, the year he was almost a high school football champion, comes to stay with him.

One day Pedro decides to run for class president, then panics when he learns that the popular Summer Wheatly (Haylie Duff) is his opponent. While Napoleon and Deb help Pedro campaign in school, Kip's online girlfriend, the very urban Lafawnduh Lucas (Shondrella Avery), arrives for a visit. Under

With his frizzy hair, buckteeth, and large eyeglasses, the title character of 2004's Napoleon Dynamite (played by Jon Heder) exemplifies the nerdy social outcast. The low budget film was a surprise hit at the box office.

Lafawnduh's loving influence Kip is transformed into an unlikely "gangsta" hipster.

At the same time Napoleon secretly teaches himself to disco dance. Napoleon's dancing skills save the day when Pedro learns that he must present a skit as part of his election speech. Napoleon's uninhibited performance wows the student body and ensures Pedro's victory. Though still very much the nerd, a more confident Napoleon looks forward to happier times with Deb as the story closes.

Production Design—Location as Character

Napoleon Dynamite is as much a story about Preston, Idaho, as it is a tale of misfit teenagers. Although the decision to shoot in Preston may have been based on finances, the impact of the location was immense. The old-fashioned, rural town echoed perfectly the movie's quirky but ordinary characters. After the film's release, fans of the movie began flocking to Preston, eager to see the places the movie was shot.

Hess and production designer Cory Lorenzen devised their exterior locations from existing structures. Many scenes in the movie open with a shot of a character standing in front of his or her home. Each home has its own style and personality and is reflective of the characters who live in it. The Dynamites' red-brick, single-story house is small and, like grandma, a little rundown around the edges. Pedro lives in an equally modest adobe house, the only Spanish style building seen in the picture. By contrast,

LOCATION SHOOTING

Location shooting—any filming that takes place outside of a studio set—can occur on any type of film or TV show. Filming locations may be mere blocks from the home studio or be thousands of miles away in another country. Entire movies may be shot on location, though most productions involve a combination of set and location filming.

Location filming has been around since the earliest silent films. Though its use waned some in the 1930s, 1940s, and 1950s, when sound and other technical issues made filming outside the studio more challenging, it has always been an important option for filmmakers. Today, filmmakers must decide whether the artistic advantages of location shooting outweigh the added costs and loss of control that can result. Sometimes constructing sets from scratch is actually cheaper.

The job of compiling a list of possible locations for filming belongs to the location scout. After determining what type of place is needed for each scene, scouts compile a list of possible locations and travel around with the production designer to select shooting sites. Usually several locations for each setting are researched, documented, and presented to the director.

Once a location has been secured, the design team determines how much modification is needed to make it work for the given scene. Very rarely are selected locations "shooting ready." Quite often, walls need to be repainted, furniture replaced, and surfaces re-dressed. Sometimes a location will undergo an extreme makeover. For one scene in *Walk the Line*, production designer David Bomba transformed a modern casino in Tunica, Mississippi, into a swanky 1960s hotel in Las Vegas. Many movies and television shows are set in one location but filmed in another. The TV show *Smallville*, for example, is set in Kansas but filmed in Vancouver, Canada.

the homes of the popular girls are manicured and upscale. Rico lives and works out of a 1974 burnt-orange Dodge conversion van, the perfect vehicle for a man who dreams of traveling back in time to revisit his youth.

Surrounding the homes are vast pastures and fields, ringed in the distance by mountains. Nothing in the town, from the diner to the bus depot, appears new. As these views suggest, Preston is an isolated place. Despite the presence of television, movies, and the Internet, the town seems trapped in another era, hopelessly out-of-date. Preston, like Napoleon and his friends, is a sweet oddity.

Space and Set Décor

In sharp contrast to Preston's expansive outdoors, the interior spaces of *Napoleon Dynamite* are boxy and insular, with low ceilings. For the tall and lanky Napoleon these tight spaces seem especially confining and oppressive.

Set décor in *Napoleon Dynamite* is understated and realistic, though every interior location is thoughtfully dressed. Thanks to grandma, Napoleon's home is a tidy homage to the prefab 1970s, complete with wood paneling, flowery couch, animal skins, wall-mounted corded phone, artificial plants, and cheesy photo portraits of Napoleon and Kip. Only the presence of Kip's computer gives away the actual time period of the story.

Pedro's home, on the other hand, is decorated with religious paintings, votive candles, and other Catholic-Mexican touches. Probably the most distinctive decorative element of Preston High School is its bright

The retro attire of the high school students at the dance symbolize the old-fashioned ways of Preston, Idaho. Center: Tina Majorino and Jon Heder.

red, orange, and blue lockers, colorful touches in an otherwise drab, institutional setting. Handmade signs are plastered across their front, breaking up the repetitive color scheme and adding a touch of teenage spontaneity.

Costumes and Make-up—Mutations and Transformations

As conceived by Jerusha Hess, make-up artist Steve Costanza, and hairstylist Daniel Demke, the costumes and make-up in *Napoleon Dynamite* stand out as key visual components in the development of the film's story.

Napoleon's super-nerd appearance—oversized glasses, wild curly hair, animal-themed teeshirts, high-waisted, beltless pants, and scuffed moonboots—required some thought on the filmmakers' part. "We were concerned because he's [Heder] a handsome guy and he dresses very well, so we were like, 'How do we get Jon Heder not to look like Jon Heder? and my wife said, 'We've got to get that man a perm.' So we got him a perm with the tightest rollers that they make. Permed his hair, gave him a nice part down the side, put him in a pair of my old moonboots, and there you go."[6]

From his hair to his shoes, Napoleon's appearance says as much about his character as his words and actions do. From his first onscreen moment, standing in his front yard waiting for the school bus, viewers know they are dealing with an oddball.

In an adolescent world where appearances count for everything, the audience can see immediately that Napoleon is a zero. Later, when he dons a suit and tie for a school dance, he strides with a power and pride that can only come with confident dressing.

Brother Kip's look is more conservative than Napoleon's but equally nerdy—polo shirts buttoned to the top, belted shorts, mid-calf socks, and slip-on canvas shoes. Kip's love-induced makeover is conveyed almost entirely through his clothes—flashy jewelry, head scarf, oversized jean jacket, etc.

Like his van, Uncle Rico's hairstyle and clothes recall the 1970s. Rico, the over-the-hill football star, favors short-sleeved, polyester pullovers and vests that show off his biceps and matching, tight-fitting pants. His side-parted hair sports the blow-dried disco look popular in his youth.

Though their clothes are distinctive—Pedro often wears Mexican-style ties and shirts and Deb dresses in overly coordinated casual wear—Deb and Pedro express themselves most strongly through their hair. When first seen, Deb wears an extreme side ponytail with color-coordinated bands, underscoring both her eccentricity and her need for style. In later scenes, Deb's ponytail shifts to the top of her head, her hair cascading out like a fountain. By the last scenes, after her connection to Napoleon is complete, the ponytail has disappeared, replaced by a flattering straight cut.

Pedro, who enjoys being the only boy in school with facial hair, displays his anxiety at having to campaign against Summer by running home and shaving his hair off. Embarrassed by his impulsive act, he then buys a cheap woman's wig supplied by Deb and wears it to school. Like Deb and her ponytails, Pedro's wig serves as both a symbol of his nonconformity and an improbable defense against rejection.

CAREERS IN PRODUCTION, COSTUME, AND MAKE-UP DESIGN

Production designers come with a variety of backgrounds and strengths, including theater, fine arts, animation, music, and architecture, but most have at least some training in the visual arts. According to production designer Lawrence G. Paull, "You need to have some sort of artistic background, be it painting, drawing, decorating, designing, or architecture. Yet, I know there are production designers who were carpenters. I know one who was a greensman on sets."[1]

Although formal education is always beneficial, there are other routes to a production design career. Before he became a production designer, Guy Hendrix Dyas (*The Brothers Grimm; X2:*

X-Men United), applied his studies in industrial design to designing Sony Walkmans and Discmans.[2] Jeannine Oppewall's first experience was in theater, where she worked as an actor, a lighting designer, and a technician. After coming to Los Angeles, she was a location manager and an art director prior to being hired as a production designer.[3]

As Paull notes, not all production designers have strong training in the arts. Currently on the faculty at New York University, Kristi Zea (*Manchurian Candidate*; *The Departed*), started out as a journalist. This led to styling photo shoots, from there to designing costumes, and finally to production design.

GETTING INTO COSTUME

Like Zea, costume designer Carol Ramsey detoured on her way to becoming a costume designer. While she earned a graduate degree in harpsichord and early music performance, she supported herself sewing and making costumes. "In the Boston Shakespeare Company costume shop I was a stitcher, and I started working with the designers. . . . I worked for a lot of years in the theater. I was married to a filmmaker, and I was doing a lot of documentary sound recording and editing soundtracks. And then it all just sort of morphed into costume designing."[4]

Choosing practicality over art, Albert Wolsky (*All That Jazz; The Road to Perdition*) worked for his father's travel business after college. He was almost thirty when he realized: "I love clothes and I love theater—why not become a costume designer?"[5]

According to Holly Cole and Kristin Burke, film costume designers are used to training people on the job. "If you're smart, fun to work with, learn quickly, and have an ardent desire to work in film, dig in and get started . . . it takes a whole lot more than just talent to make it in this field."[6]

Costume designer Rita Ryack (*A Beautiful Mind*; *The Cat in the Hat*) agrees: "I think it's good to go out and see the world and try all kinds of things before you settle down to a career. The more references you have . . . the better you can tell a story."[7]

GETTING INTO MAKE-UP

Special effects make-up artist Howard Berger was drawn to the field from an early age. "When I was very, very young, my father took me to see some of the *Planet of the Apes* movies, and that's where I really got hooked."[8] Berger believes that aspiring make-up artists should have a calling for the field. "Don't get into this because you think you're going to make tons of money, or you're going to be in magazines or articles or become famous. Get into this because you love movies and you love creatures and make-up . . . Be up for any task and don't turn anything down."[9]

TO SCHOOL, OR NOT TO SCHOOL

Although formal education after high school is not required to get work as a production designer, costume designer, or make-up artist, schools can

Choosing a Make-up School

Make-up artists can work as personal stylists, special effects make-up artists, in theater, television, music videos, and films. Before choosing a school, a prospective make-up artist should determine if the school offers courses in the area of interest.

Some additional questions to ask when shopping for a make-up school:

1. Is the school accredited or licensed?
2. What is the school's current reputation?
3. Who are the instructors and what relevant experience do they have?
4. What is the curriculum?
5. How much will the course and the materials cost?
6. What is the student to instructor ratio?
7. What are the facilities like?
8. What is the proportion of time spent doing actual hands-on application?
9. What products do I receive in my make-up kit and classroom materials?
10. Does the school have recent successful graduates?
11. Is mentoring offered?
12. Does the school bring in recognized guest instructors and speakers?
13. Does the school offer job placement assistance?

teach techniques and develop talents. They can also be a source of contacts in the industry. "Mentors are very, very, very important," insists Jeanine Oppewall, who worked with all-around designer Charles Eames before she began her film career.[10]

Mentors were instrumental in helping many of today's special effects make-up artists get their start. At age fourteen, Rob Bottin (*Mission: Impossible*; *Fight Club*) submitted illustrations to special effects make-up artist Rick Baker. Bottin later worked with Baker until he got his first solo film, *The Howling*, whose groundbreaking, low-budget transformation effects put him on the map. Similarly, Howard Berger contacted his idols, who eventually "kind of took me under their wing."[11]

Formal training is not that important to success as a costume designer, according to Deena Appel. "I think it's important to be enormously resourceful, and to study a lot of films that tell you the story through costumes, to really understand that it's not about glamour and the beautiful people."[12]

Many film and theater schools offer courses in production, costume, or make-up design, but as is apparent from the comments above, there are many different ways to acquire skills in these fields. Some, such as make-up artist John Goodwin, strongly believe that an overall film education is the best preparation for working in any aspect of the industry.[13] Programs that emphasize the theater instead of film can also be good preparation. As Judianna Makovsky says, "You should go and try and work in theater. It will teach you how to problem solve."[14]

GETTING AN EDUCATION IN ART DIRECTION

The following institutions offer classes or degrees in production design as part of their general film or theater studies programs:

- California Institute of the Arts, School of Theater
- Chapman University
- Los Angeles Film School
- New York University, Tisch School of the Arts
- North Carolina School of the Arts
- Ohio University, School of Theater
- Oklahoma City University
- Rhode Island School of Design
- University of California, Los Angeles, School of Theater, Film and Television
- University of Southern California, School of Cinematic Arts

Some schools that offer classes in costume design for film or theater or costume design programs are:

- California Institute for the Arts, School of Theater
- California State University, Long Beach, Extension Services
- DePaul University, The Theater School
- Fashion Institute of Design and Merchandising
- Los Angeles City College Theater Academy

- New York University, Tisch School of the Arts
- Otis Art Institute
- Parsons The New School for Design
- Purdue University
- University of California, Irvine
- University of California, Los Angeles
- University of Florida, School of Theater and Dance

No formal education beyond high school is required to become a professional make-up artist in the United States, but experience in cosmetology or in theater is recommended.

Some schools that offer training in make-up are:

- Academy of Cosmetic Arts
- California State University, Fullerton
- Cinema Make-up School
- Douglas Education Center (Tom Savini's Special Make-up Effects Program)
- EI School of Professional Make-up
- Elegance International Academy of Professional Make-up
- Empire Academy of Make-up
- Joe Blasco Make-up Center West, Inc.
- Libs Theatrical Make-up School
- Make-up Designory, New York and Los Angeles
- New York University, Tisch School of the Arts
- North Carolina Schools of the Arts
- The Studio Make-up Academy
- The Skin & Make-up Institute of Arizona
- Westmore Academy of Cosmetic Arts

SALARIES

In general, salaries for jobs in art direction vary depending on the overall budget of the project. A big-budget theatrical feature will pay significantly more than a low-budget cable show, but network television and some high-end cable producers, like HBO, will pay much better than a low-budget feature. Whether the production is "union" (i.e., the production company making the project is a signatory of the various movie unions and guilds) also impacts salary.

The range of salaries within the production design team is as broad as the skills represented. Some members, such as carpenters, may belong to unions that have their own pay scales. Most costume

ART DIRECTOR SALARIES (GUILD RATES)

Starting Salary	Experienced Salary	"Star" Salary
As low as $2,100 per week	$2,800 per week	Six figures

COSTUME DESIGNER SALARIES (GUILD RATES)

Starting Salary	Experienced Salary	"Star" Salary
As low as $2,000 per week	$5,000 a week for films	Six figures

MAKE-UP ARTISTS AND HAIRSTYLISTS SALARIES

Starting Salary	Experienced Salary	"Star" Salary
As low as $18 an hour	$35–40 an hour	Name your own price

designers start off working on low-budget films to build up their resumes. Often they receive little or no salary above their costume budget. Once they have enough experience to join the Costume Designers Guild, they earn at least the guild minimum. Like many people in the entertainment industry, costume designers are independent agents. The most successful are sought out for major projects and can negotiate higher salaries for themselves. Others may work only sporadically, making good money one year and little or none the next.

Make-up artists and hairstylists work long hours— a minimum of fourteen hours a day for film and sixteen hours a day for television. Beginning make-up artists and hairstylists are paid very little, but make up for their low salaries by gaining valuable on-the-job training. A few make-up artists, especially those working in special effects make-up, can name their own price.

GLOSSARY

allegorical—Representing abstract ideas or principles with characters in a dramatic or narrative form such as a play, movie, or book.

animatronic—A remote-controlled system that uses mechanical devices to produce a life-like performance using puppets or models.

bald cap—A close-fitting, thin plastic, rubber, or foam latex cap applied to an actor to make it look as if he or she were bald.

blue screen process—An optical process by which subjects filmed in front of a blue screen are combined with a separately filmed background. In addition to blue screen, digital processes can use a surface painted green or any other consistent color.

character make-up—Make-up intended to change an actor's age, race, or facial or body shape.

cinematographer—Devises the photographic look of a movie and films the story's action.

close-up—When a character or object is drawn or photographed from a short distance. In a close-up, the subject of the shot will fill most of the frame.

computer graphics (CG)—Any changes that are made to film images using digital equipment and computers.

contouring—The application of shades and colors to the face or body to define or subtly change shapes.

costume designer—Creates garments that capture and define characters in a film and advance the film's story. Supervises costume requirements and hiring and firing of support personnel, and is responsible for delivering costumes on time and on budget.

costume illustrator—Draws costume designs in consultation with the costume designer for presentation to the director, producer, pattern makers, tailors, and seamstresses.

costume supervisor—Manages and supervises the costume department's day-to-day operations, including keeping the budget, assembling costume stock, and supervising wardrobe preparation.

costumer—Dresses the actors and maintains the costumes.

décor—Style of decoration, as of a room or building.

distressing—Dyeing, sanding, airbrushing, and otherwise treating costumes so that they look old.

Edwardian—The period from 1901 to 1910 that coincides with the reign of King Edward VII in the United Kingdom. At this time, rapid industrialization resulted in more social mobility. Clothing was looser and more flexible than during the rigid Victorian era that preceded it.

ensemble—A cast in which most of the actors have roles of equal importance.

expressionism—A style of filmmaking that distorts time and space and emphasizes basic qualities of people and objects.

fish skin—A thin, transparent skin originally intended for medical purposes, that was used in early make-up.

flexible collodian—A liquid plastic skin adhesive used by early make-up artists to create wrinkles, scars, and burn marks.

foam latex—A special latex mixture that can be molded for use in prosthetics.

foundation—A skin-colored, light-reflecting make-up that provides a base for color and contouring.

gray scale—Color values between black and white.

greasepaint—A mixture of grease and colorings used in theatrical make-up.

hairstylist—The person responsible for designing and maintaining actors' hair during filming. Works with the make-up designer to ensure that hairstyles are appropriate for the characters and period.

hue—A gradation or variety of a color.

latex—A natural rubber that comes in several thicknesses. Applied as a liquid, it dries in semi-solid form. It is used in special effects and aging make-up to create wrinkles, wounds, burns, and bald caps, among other things.

laying on hair—Applying loose hair directly to the body or face.

luminance—The brightness of a light source or an illuminated surface.

make-up artist—The person who applies make-up to actors for cosmetic purposes and to help create characters.

matte shot—An image that combines blue or green screen process or a digital image with live-action footage.

old-age stipple—A mixture of gum latex, powder, gelatin, and ground-up pancake make-up. It can be dried and stretched to produce realistic wrinkles and rough skin textures to make actors appear older than they are.

palette—The range of colors used by a particular artist.

pancake make-up—A grease-free cake make-up used for covering large areas.

perspective—The illusion of depth, as rendered on a two-dimensional surface.

production designer—Also called the art director, creates the physical world behind the action, as interpreted by the director.

prosthetics—Materials, including foam latex, rubber, plastic, and gelatin, that are molded and applied to the face or body to change their shape or appearance. They can be as small as a nosepiece or as large as entire suits.

saturated color—Color with the highest intensity of hue; absence of white.

scale—The relative size of objects within a setting.

set decorations—The décor, props, and furnishings that fill out a set or location.

special effects make-up—Make-up that goes beyond simply changing the character's look with color. It usually involves prosthetics of some kind and includes bullet wounds, injuries, blood, and fantasy and science fiction characters.

spectrum—Series of colors.

squib—An electrical firing device that creates the appearance of an explosion. A blood bag placed over a squib is used to simulate a bullet hit.

straight make-up—Make-up applied to define and enhance the face and to correct imperfections.

stunt double—Actors who substitute for stars when they are unable or unwilling to perform dangerous or difficult actions.

tint—A hue to which white has been added.

value—How light or dark a hue appears when compared to neighboring hues on the spectrum.

volume—The total size of a space.

wash—Thinned down make-up tints used for various purposes.

CHAPTER NOTES

INTRODUCTION

1. Deborah Nadoolman Landis, *Screencraft: Costume Design* (Burlington, Mass.: Focal Press, 2003), p. 8.

CHAPTER 1. PRODUCTION DESIGN

1. Vincent LoBrutto, *By Design: Interviews with Film Production Designers* (Westport, Conn.: Praeger Publishers, 1992), p. 177.

2. Ibid., p. 194.

3. Ibid., p. 85.

4. Ward Preston, *What an Art Director Does: An Introduction to Motion Picture Production Design* (Los Angeles: Silman-James Press, 1994), p. 75.

5. "PBS Hollywood Presents: The Old Settler, In-Depth Interview, John Iacovelli: The Production Designer In-Depth, The Design Process," n.d., <http://www.pbs.org/hollywoodpresents/theoldsettler/indepth/id_pd_1.html> (June 30, 2006).

6. LoBrutto, p. 8.

7. Preston, p. 107.

8. Ibid., p. 85.

9. Transcript archive, "Herman Zimmerman (Production Designer)," Startrek.com, October 16, 1997,

<http://www.startrek.com/startrek/view/community/ chat/archive/transcript/1436.html> (September 14, 2006).

Chapter 2. Costume and Make-up Design

1. "Chat Transcript: Costume Designer Talks About Creating 'Austin Powers,'" CNN.com, July 6, 1999, <http://www.cnn.com/STYLE/9907/06/appel. transcript/> (May 29, 2006).

2. Holly Cole and Kristin Burke, *Costuming for Film: The Art and the Craft* (Los Angeles: Silman-James Press, 2005), pp. 151–152.

3. Sophie de Rakoff, "Women in Hollywood 2005: Sophie de Rakoff," *Premiere* Magazine, n.d., <http:// www.premiere.com/features/2333/sophie-de-rakoff.html> (June 4, 2006).

4. Cole, p. 82.

5. Author interview with Jane Ruhm, July 2, 2006.

6. Rebecca Murray, "Greg Nicotero on Land of the Dead, George Romero, and Creating Zombies," *Your Guide to Hollywood Movies*, June 21, 2005, <http:// movies.about.com/od/landofthedead/a/deadgn062105. htm> (May 29, 2006).

7. Michael Mallory, "Steve LaPorte Gets in His Work," *Make-Up Artist*, February/March 2005, p. 46.

8. Davida Simon, "Hey, This Isn't Reality!" Themakeuproom.com, 2003, <http://www. themakeuproom.com/ Reality_andthe_movies.html> (May 29, 2006).

9. Vincent J-R Kehoe, *The Technique of the Professional Make-Up Artist for Film, Television and Stage* (Boston: Focal Press, 1985), p. 91.

10. Michael F. Blake, *Lon Chaney: The Man Behind the Thousand Faces* (Vestal, NY: Vestal Press, 1993), pp. 182–183.

11. Michael Key, "Click: Getting Better with Age," *Make-up Artist*, May/June 2006, p. 40.

12. Ibid., p. 38.

13. Mallory, p. 45.

CHAPTER 3. PUTTING IT ALL TOGETHER: PERIOD FILMS

1. "Elizabethan Fashion and Times," reproduced from the *Shakespeare in Love* Miramax press kit, n.d.,<http://members.tripod.com/~firthpage/rolespage/silfash.html> (July 21, 2006).

2. Ibid.

3. Ibid.

4. Ibid.

5. Ibid.

6. Ibid.

7. Ibid.

8. "*Seabiscuit*: Production Notes," Cinema.com, n.d., <http://www.cinema.com/articles/2366/seabiscuit-production-notes.phtml> (February 8, 2007).

9. Scott Essman, "The Art of Cinematic Design," *MovieMaker Magazine*, issue 35, September/October 1999, <http://www.moviemaker.com/magazine/editorial.php?id=423> (February 7, 2007).

10. Production Design: Case Studies seminar, Jeannine Oppewall, Academy of Motion Picture Arts and Sciences, April 14, 2004.

11. *Seabiscuit*: Production notes.

12. Hirsh.

13. "The Art of Writing and Making Films: *The New World*," The Writing Studio, n.d., <http://www.writingstudio.co.za/page864.html> (February 8, 2007).

14. John Calhoun, "From the Bard to Bowie, Sandy Powell Dresses Up Three New Releases," *Live Design*, n.d., <http://livedesignonline.com/ar/show_business_bard_bowie_sandy/> (August 26, 2006).

15. Press notes for *Cinderella Man*, n.d., p. 29.

16. *Seabiscuit*: Production notes.

17. Ibid.

18. Todd Longwell, Randee Dawn, and Sheigh Crabtree, "Crafts I: The Look," *Hollywood Reporter*, February 9, 2004, <http://www.hollywoodreporter.com/thr/film/feature_display.jsp?vnu_content_id=2089246> (August 23, 2006).

Chapter 4. Putting It All Together: Science Fiction, Horror, and Fantasy Films

1. Vincent LoBrutto, *By Design: Interviews With Film Production Designers* (Westport, Conn.: Praeger Publishers, 1992), pp. 171–172.

2. Ibid., p. 170.

3. Ibid., p. 171.

4. Ibid., p. 172.

5. Paul M. Sammon, *Future Noir: The Making of Blade Runner* (New York: HarperCollins, 1996), pp. 73–74.

6. LoBrutto, p. 172.

7. Paul M. Sammon, "Future Noir: The Making of Blade Runner, Chapter VIII—The Crew," deleted material, n.d., <http://scribble.com/uwi/br/fn/fn-ch8.html> (August 30, 2006).

8. C. S. Lewis, "It All Began as a Picture," *Of Other Worlds: Essays and Stories*, ed. Walter Hooper (London: Geoffrey Blis, 1966).

9. Perry Moore, *The Chronicles of Narnia: The Lion, the Witch and the Wardrobe: The Official Illustrated Movie Companion* (New York: Harper Collins, 2005), p. 138.

10. Ellen Wolff, "Separating Narnia from Middle Earth," *Daily Variety*, January 10, 2006, p. A8.

11. Production notes, *The Chronicles of Narnia: The Lion, the Witch and the Wardrobe.*

12. Moore, p. 144.

13. Tan Lee Kuen, "Mussenden's Costume Magic," *The Star Online*, November 26, 2005, <http://star-ecentral.com/news/story.asp?file=/2005/11/26/movies/12671659&sec=movies> (July 27, 2006).

14. "On Location With *The Chronicles of Narnia: The Lion, the Witch and the Wardrobe*," *The Star Online*, July 18, 2005, <http://star-ecentral.com/narnia/story.asp?file=/2005/7/18/narnia/20050718181952&sec=narnia> (July 5, 2006).

15. "*The Chronicles of Narnia: The Lion, the Witch and the Wardrobe*," *Make-Up Artist*, December 2005/January 2006, p. 36.

16. Pascal Pinteau, *Special Effects: An Oral History: Interviews with 38 Masters Spanning 100 Years* (New York: Henry N. Abrams, 2004), p. 309.

17. Adena Halpern, "Magic Year for Makeup," *Daily Variety*, February 14, 2002, p. A1.

18. Joe Nazzaro, "Creating Narnia: KNB Takes on the Fantasy World of C. S. Lewis, in *The Lion, the Witch and the Wardrobe*," *Make-up Artist,* p. 73.

19. Ibid., p. 66.

CHAPTER 5. PUTTING IT ALL TOGETHER: CONTEMPORARY FILMS

1. Steven Kotler, "Eye on the Oscars: The Director: Paul Haggis, *Crash*," *Variety,* December 6, 2005, p. A6.

2. Production Notes, *Crash*.

3. Linda Bass, speaking to a high school class, 2006.

4. Kotler.

5. Author interview with Linda Bass.

6. Wendy Mitchell, "Geeks Shall Inherit the Earth; Jared Hess Talks About *Napoleon Dynamite*," n.d., <http://www.indiewire.com/people/people_040609hess.html> (September 3, 2006).

CHAPTER 6. CAREERS IN PRODUCTION, COSTUME, AND MAKE-UP DESIGN

1. Vincent LoBrutto, *By Design: Interviews With Film Production Designers* (Westport, Conn.: Praeger Publishers, 1992), p. 178.

2. "Next Gen Crafts: Production Design," *Hollywood Reporter,* February 12, 2004, <http://www. hollywoodreporter.com (September 4, 2006).

3. Production Design seminar.

4. Costume Design seminar.

5. Deborah Nadoolman Landis, *Screencraft: Costume Design* (Burlington, Mass.: Focal Press, 2003), p. 163.

6. Cole and Burke, p. 24.

7. Costume Design seminar.

8. Evan Jacobs, "Exclusive Interview: Talking Makeup With *The Chronicles of Narnia*'s Howard Berger," Movieweb.com, n.d., <http://www.movieweb. com/dvd/news/06/11706.php> (July 10, 2006).

9. Ibid.

10. Production Design seminar.

11. Jacobs.

12. "Chat Transcript: Costume Designer Talks About Creating 'Austin Powers,'" with Deena Appel, CNN.com, July 6, 1999, <http://www.cnn.com/ STYLE/9907/06/appel.transcript/> (February 8, 2007).

13. John Goodwin, "Nothing Stands Alone: The Importance of Learning About Filmmaking," *Make-Up Artist*, October/November 2005, p. 30.

14. Costume Design seminar.

FURTHER READING

Books

Cole, Holly and Kristin Burke. *Costuming for Film: The Art and the Craft*. Los Angeles: Silman-James Press, 2005.

LoBrutto, Vincent. *The Filmmakers Guide to Production Design*. New York: Allworth Press, 2002.

Musgrove, Jan. *Make-up, Hair and Costume for Film and Television*. Boston: Focal Press, 2003.

Rizzo, Michael. *The Art Direction Handbook for Film*. Boston: Focal Press, 2005.

Internet Addresses

Artdirectors.org
http://www.artdirectors.org

Make-Up Artist Magazine online
http://www.makeupmag.com

INDEX